I've been waiting for this book to be written for a long time. In *Asking Better Questions of the Bible*, Marty Solomon gives us a treasure map to uncover riches in the Bible by taking the reader back to the Hebraic context of the ancient world. You'll never read the Bible the same way after going through this book.

ROBBY GALLATY, pastor of Long Hollow Church and author of *The Forgotten Jesus* and *Growing Up*

This book is, above all else, an invitation. It's an invitation to bring our whole selves to our reading of Scripture, confident that doing so will lead us into a deeper level of meaning and understanding. Solomon asks us to join him on a journey away from easy answers and toward a richer encounter not only with the biblical text itself but, more importantly, with the God who beckons us to draw near. For anyone committed to discipleship, this is an invitation to enthusiastically accept.

JENNIFER ROSNER, affiliate assistant professor of systematic theology at Fuller Theological Seminary and author of *Finding Messiah*

Marty helps us see that asking questions about the Bible shouldn't make us nervous; instead, it can usher us into new possibilities in our relationship with God and his Word. By diving deep in fresh and engaging ways, this book will help you experience the goodness of God in what's revealed in Scripture—and help you fall in love with Jesus for the first time . . . again.

J.R. BRIGGS, founder of Kairos Partnei
The Sacred Overlap

T0053986

Asking Better Questions of the Bible is for everyone who loves the Bible—or who *wants* to love the Bible but has been wounded by those using it as a weapon. With a writing voice as knowledgeable as a seminary prof and as accessible as a close friend, Marty Solomon provides the tools you need to find the God of goodness and love in these ancient pages. Whether this is your first or fiftieth time looking for God in the Bible, I urge you to pick up a copy of this book and find hope, life, and the freedom to imagine better questions.

    CATHERINE McNIEL, author of *Fearing Bravely*

If you find the bestselling book of all time—the Bible—irrelevant, inaccurate, or insignificant, you're not alone, but you may want to reconsider. Marty's latest offers both a nuanced and a faithful way to reimagine the text as both sacred and transformational. Read this book for tools and insights that will help you reclaim the bestselling book of all time.

    AJ SHERRILL, Anglican priest and author of *Being with God*

This book is an invitation to a deeper truth and a better approach to applying it. There is so much in this book for small groups, discipling one-on-one, or even teaching from the stage. All followers of Jesus will be inspired to examine how we talk about what we talk about.

    AARON COUCH, MA, pastor at Southeast Christian Church

Well, I'll be . . . Marty did it. He *actually* wrote a balanced, inviting, captivating book about the Bible. It is lively but not cheap. It is rigorous but not punishing. It is faithful but not fideistic. This book deepens the faith-giving approach to the Bible that so many of us have found in *The BEMA Podcast*. And, thank God, it's readable!

PETER HARTWIG, MDIV, lecturer at WTC Theology

In *Asking Better Questions of the Bible*, Marty Solomon offers wonderful examples and resources for doing precisely what the title suggests while inviting the reader to engage the Hebrew context and the distinctions between Eastern and Western thought. This alone is worth the price of the book and is desperately needed in modern biblical interpretation. *Asking Better Questions of the Bible* is a gem for those desiring to be shaped by the Text as opposed to simply deconstructing it. It offers a refined set of tools for a deepening relationship with the Bible and the God it reveals.

BRIAN HARDIN, visionary and voice of the Daily Audio Bible

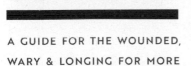

ASKING
BETTER
QUESTIONS
OF THE
BIBLE

A GUIDE FOR THE WOUNDED,
WARY & LONGING FOR MORE

MARTY SOLOMON

NavPress®

*A NavPress resource published in alliance
with Tyndale House Publishers*

NavPress is the publishing ministry of The Navigators, an international Christian organization and leader in personal spiritual development. NavPress is committed to helping people grow spiritually and enjoy lives of meaning and hope through personal and group resources that are biblically rooted, culturally relevant, and highly practical.

For more information, visit NavPress.com.

Asking Better Questions of the Bible: A Guide for the Wounded, Wary, and Longing for More

Copyright © 2023 by Marty Solomon. All rights reserved.

A NavPress resource published in alliance with Tyndale House Publishers

NavPress and the NavPress logo are registered trademarks of NavPress, The Navigators, Colorado Springs, CO. *Tyndale* is a registered trademark of Tyndale House Ministries. Absence of ® in connection with marks of NavPress or other parties does not indicate an absence of registration of those marks.

The Team:
David Zimmerman, Publisher; Caitlyn Carlson, Acquisitions Editor; Elizabeth Schroll, Copy Editor; Olivia Eldredge, Operations Manager; Libby Dykstra, Designer and Illustrator; Sarah K. Johnson, Proofreader

Cover illustration by Libby Dykstra. Copyright © 2023 by NavPress/The Navigators. All rights reserved. Cover photograph of chipboard texture copyright © Retro Supply Co. All rights reserved.

Author photo by Brent Billings, copyright © 2020. All rights reserved.

Published in association with The Bindery Agency, TheBinderyAgency.com

For information about special discounts for bulk purchases, please contact Tyndale House Publishers at csresponse@tyndale.com, or call 1-855-277-9400.

ISBN 978-1-64158-570-5

Printed in the United States of America

29	28	27	26	25	24	23
7	6	5	4	3		

This is dedicated to Graham and Raylene Solomon.
To Mom, for teaching me the two most
important things in all the cosmos.
To Dad.
I am so unbelievably proud of you.
And I'm proud to be your son.

Contents

CHAPTER 1

SEEING THE TEXT IN CONTEXT

The Case for Inspiration

I am deeply convicted that the Bible is the inspired Word of God.

For those familiar with my work, that may seem like a strange opening line for this book. I'm a teacher who passionately encourages people to think critically and ask big questions. I believe we should be free to doubt and let those doubts carry us into deeper wonder and curiosity. Our doubts shouldn't scare us. But neither should we embrace them as a place to settle, a permanent state of being. Doubts are invitations, opportunities to continue the journey of discovery.

That's why I try to cultivate a kind of learning space, a place where doubts are welcome and find a voice. It's why

I talk about overlooked historical context or the cultural assumptions that could be driving the biblical conversation. I love to examine the theories put forward by academic experts who have given their lives to studying these details. Questions invigorate my study.

Many of these experts probably wouldn't share my commitment to the Scripture's inspiration. The world of textual criticism can be a cold, analytical place. But here is what I know: The discoveries and proposals I have found make the Scriptures come alive and burst with color. As we search through the data, pondering the conclusions (and doubts) of others, considering things that may seem off-limits at first—that practice, far from driving us from "the truth," further reinforces the power and beauty of the Text (what I often call the Bible). We become people who take God's Word more seriously when we think through and grapple with the implications of these ideas.

I know that, for many, this journey is laden with insecurity and causes us to wonder whether we are questioning too much. But God has always honored and respected those who refuse to let go. Even when the wrestling results in a limp (recall Jacob the Wrestler of Genesis), it also brings about a new identity that carries us—and generations after us—through the story with more intimacy and vibrancy in our faithfulness. Our wrestling can make us more convinced, not less, of the Bible's inspiration.

But too often in the church, we have turned the rich reality of inspiration into a means of settling—for easy answers, pseudosecurity, self-assurance, or false resolution. When I was growing up, the Word was used too quickly and defensively.

I understand why. The entire human experience is one long battle with fear and insecurity. One of the things we desire more than anything else is to *know*—to sense that we have arrived, that at least for a moment we can take a deep breath and just relax. As Brené Brown points out, research shows that our brains reward themselves for completing a story loop.[1] In other words, when we bring a plot or a conflict to resolution, our brains get a bit of a dopamine boost. This is part of what it means to be human, and compassionately understanding that about ourselves is a beautiful thing.

But we also ought to note the dangers that lie in this reality. Our biological and psychological processes are wired to look for those resolutions, whether they are real or not. There's a reward for finding them, but some of the treasures are fool's gold.

When it comes to our beliefs about God and faith—the things that are so foundational to who we are—we begin to feel anxious at the gravity of our questions. We move quickly toward the safety and allure of resolution. If we question the bedrock to which we have anchored our identity and our eternity, we can easily feel like we are falling. The quicker we can reconstruct that foundation, the more secure we feel.

And so we stop too soon. We take the off-ramp, settling for something just short of the real and liberating payoff. Like the Israelites at the bitter well of Marah, we set up shop and build our theologies rather than pushing ahead and finding

Elim—a beautiful place with twelve wells and seventy palm trees—just around the corner (see Exodus 15:22-27).

I know because I've been there. It's where I found myself as a young Bible college student and then as a pastor. Quick explanations. Confident declarations. Slick and polished theology.

But the fact of the matter was that I had seen too much. The very constructs that pushed me toward easy answers also required me to know the Scriptures—and I'd spent too much time in the Bible for those answers and explanations to satisfy. I didn't say it out loud, but I had so many questions and doubts.

I have spent so much time deconstructing my experience as a child raised in Christian subculture. But on this point, I need to express some gratitude to my fundamentalist evangelical parents—because that was the context where I first became convinced of the importance of two things: Jesus and the Bible.

I'm not sure where you're at as you read these pages, but if you're anything like me, and anything like the people who join me on *The BEMA Podcast*, you might be feeling a little shaky right about now. You want to love Jesus. You want to trust the Bible. But it may be that there's too much muddy water under that evangelical bridge for you to have much confidence in me when I say both are important for this journey.

That's okay. I've walked this road long enough to know

that none of us have it settled or figured out at the beginning. This matter of wrestling with God is one of the most meaningful journeys that you and I will ever embark upon. The tension can be trusted, and the content can be tested. This trust can seem counterintuitive, but when we press into the journey, we usually end up meeting the Person who holds all things together, including each of us and our frazzled faith. This Person is compassion and love incarnate and remains faithful even when we feel faithless, and he tends to find us along the way.

When I think about the relationships that matter the most to me—like the one I have with my wife or the ones with my children or my best friends—part of what makes these relationships what they are is the fact that we have been through trials together. Our relationships have been tested, but that journey has only drawn us closer. Not all relationships are like this; some don't survive the fire. But the ones that matter do—because we've fought for each other.

Nobody will fight for us more zealously, with more commitment and perseverance, with more forgiveness and compassion and love, than the One we are examining now. I can state this with such clarity and confidence because I know him. He has never left me or forsaken me. He has been a safe place for every twisted emotion and scary hurt. He has been the only One able to transform and redeem the ugliest parts of me and of the world that you and I live in.

And he has never scoffed at a single question of mine.

A WORD ABOUT JESUS

This book will be an entire discussion about the Bible: how important it is and how to read it better. But there's a crucial pit stop to make, as much for myself as for you, before we get started. We do not read the Bible in a vacuum, or in isolation, as a simple mental exercise. We do not start with knowledge for knowledge's sake. We seek to engage the Bible more faithfully because of its ability to connect us with the One who can transform all things.

I love the Bible, but the Bible is not the focus of my affection. It is not the object of my worship. The people of God worship God, not the Bible. We follow a person—his name is Jesus—whom we are to adore, imitate, submit to, and follow to the ends of the earth.

Throughout my journey of faith, I have been blessed with incredible mentors who kept talking about the person of Jesus and what he was up to. They kept helping me connect the dots of who Jesus is personally and not just what the Bible said as a head exercise. Most of them have been people who are deeply committed to prayer. They taught me how to pray and how to build a relationship with this mysterious Christ.

But prayer never came easily for me. To this day, it's not my native posture—I've never quite been able to get comfortable in that space. But because these mentors insisted on the importance of prayer, silence, solitude, listening, and fasting, I stuck with it. And these practices changed my life—because in the silence, the listening, and the intentional space for conversation, the person of Jesus became quite real to me.

Then, later in my journey, God supplied me with mentors who had a passion for the Text—and I found the expression of my faith I had been looking for all my life. Suddenly I felt like I was speaking in my native tongue. Much as prayer and contemplative practices filled the spiritual lives of my earlier mentors, the study of the Text deepened me spiritually.

I'm glad I found the first mentors first. I had been introduced not just to academic study and ideas about a special book—I had been introduced to the person of Jesus. To this day, I remain committed to those contemplative practices because they keep me tethered to a concrete relationship, not just abstract ideas—something that, for me, needs to precede the study and connects that study to the person of Christ.

I often tell my students to remember that this whole thing is about Jesus. Just Jesus.

Not "Jesus, and . . ."

Not "Jesus, as long as . . ."

Not "Jesus, but . . ."

Just Jesus.

We have to remember that all our study facilitates the bigger and better thing: our connection to the resurrected Christ. So before we start talking about the Text and the details and the literary nuances and the context and the Jewish methods, let us remember that Jesus is the guide, the destination, and the hiking partner for this adventure.

A WORD ABOUT THE BIBLE

While much about the Christian subculture I grew up in has proven to be built on shaky ground, they got this right: The Bible is necessary, valuable, and reliable for the life of faith. I knew this book was rock solid and could be trusted in its content.

The seed of this belief was what sprouted later in life when my questions wouldn't leave me alone. As I began to explore these questions with other committed believers, they would get increasingly agitated. "You don't need to ask that," they would insist. "Just trust the Bible."

But that was the thing—I *did* trust the Bible. This very trust gave me the confidence to ask questions. I suppose some folks ask questions from a place of disbelief. They don't think the Bible can be trusted, and their questions are aimed at affirming their assumptions. We often believe all doubts come from this place.

But some doubts—maybe even most of them—come from a place of confidence. Whether it's confidence in God or in the Bible, these questions are a weird mixture of assurance and humility. We don't assume that the Bible is wrong, but that it is right and we simply aren't seeing, haven't considered, or haven't discovered the whole picture. The humility of these questions sees the bigness of God, the bigness of truth, the bigness of this inspired story that's been passed down through the ages—and assumes there is so, so much more.

Of all the things I grew to distrust from my upbringing,

neither Jesus nor the Bible was ever among them. And I was ready to double down on my conviction about these things. What confused me was why most of the faithful people around me, who talked with such a tone of confidence, didn't want to do the same. It seemed like all the boisterous talk about trusting the Bible was just a façade that kept us from actually trusting the Bible.

Within the evangelical world in which I was raised, it's fashionable for people to claim they have a "high view of Scripture." *The Bible says so, and that settles it!* is a common mantra. These people believe that a simple, straightforward reading of the Bible is the most faithful way to engage with God's Word.

The "liberals," I was told (with a definite sense of disgust and disdain), were people who didn't believe in the inspiration and authority of the Bible. Their interest in cultural and historical context and anything else beyond a plain reading of the Text meant that they had a very "low" view of Scripture— and (obviously) of God and all things that are holy.

There was some truth to this. Many "liberal" scholars don't hold to the Bible's inspiration and authority; they treat it as any other piece of literature. As I've said before, I am indebted to the early lessons from the fundamentalist subculture to "simply read the Bible" and try to do what it seems to be saying.

But I couldn't shake the thought that a "simply read the Bible" approach seemed to be missing some key questions that would lead, in fact, to a more faithful engagement with the Bible. What about translations and cultural context? And which translation? Was the Bible written to me or to historical audiences? And how does this impact the inspired meaning of the Text? When we don't consider these things, don't we risk presuming that *we* are the ultimate authority—that our individual perspectives and postures are what lend the Scripture its true meaning? And isn't it readily apparent that our perspectives are wildly different from the ones the Bible assumes?

"Simply reading the Bible," it seemed, was just an easy way out. If we clung to that, we could brush off the need to ask penetrating questions about whether we are reading the Bible correctly.

And reading the Bible correctly is of immeasurable importance. The evangelical tradition hangs its worldview and behavior on what the Text is telling us. Getting the interpretation right is of utmost significance to those with a high view of Scripture.

Understanding what the Bible is saying equips us to be devoted to what it teaches us. So I realized that I needed to answer some of these better questions. And to do that, I needed to create a space where these two worlds—of devoted commitment to the Bible and of academic scholarship— overlapped, like a Venn diagram.

Isn't that what we want? "No," I was told. "Those ivory-tower academics are all just liberals trying to puff themselves up with knowledge. We figured this all out a while ago. Just trust the system." There were two problems with this. First, the characterization of academia was lazy and blatantly untrue. Second, every system we had trusted in the past had gotten things wrong—sometimes critically wrong. The very movements and traditions we were in started because of fallacies. It was inevitable that we would get things wrong as well.

And we should want to know what those things are—because we have a high view of Scripture.

Or do we?

Brian McLaren (who I had been told was a "liberal" who didn't love the Bible the right way) advocated for an even higher view of Scripture: one that doesn't settle for a simple reading of the Text but is instead so committed to the authority of the Bible that it sees the need to study the original languages and listen to historians and archaeologists about the context of Scripture.[2] All this is vital if we want to learn what the Bible is actually trying to say, not just what we *think* it is saying or what we have *wanted* it to say for centuries in our own context.

McLaren's words gave me language for my own journey. I was not looking to get rid of a high view of Scripture—but I was finding that this "high view of Scripture" *wasn't high enough*. It was, at least at times, a high view of doctrine, of dogma, and of tradition. But we were not actually committed to having a high view of Scripture itself.

My desire for a higher view of Scripture and its Author became the reason for my study.

LITERARY TOURISTS

I have a friend who likes to say, "When we ask questions the Bible isn't asking, we always get the wrong answers." Really?

Always? We *always* get the wrong answers? Yes. This doesn't mean that the answers we may find aren't good or helpful, or even accurate in some way. But *on a hermeneutical level,* when it comes to biblical interpretation, if you ask questions the Bible isn't asking, then you are asking the wrong questions. And if you're asking the wrong questions, then you are getting the wrong answers as a work of exegesis.

That's why we're embarking on this quest: to have a better understanding of what the Bible is saying or not saying; this growing understanding helps us deepen our relationship with the God of the Bible. Our goal is to understand, to the best of our ability, the inspired messages of the Text, whether they are stories, songs, genealogies, poems, letters, or visions.

Here's where I want us to start: from the assumption that the inspired meaning of the Text lies in the original conversation between author and audience. Not every hermeneutic and approach assumes this, but it makes the most logical sense to me. Some refer to this understanding as "communicative intent." Another way I've heard this expressed is "authorial intent." What this means is that we let our journey be guided by these questions:

- What did the author mean when they wrote it?
- What did the audience understand when they heard it?
- What is the inspired conversation (in the Text) trying to communicate to us?

If we do our best to understand this conversation, then we are getting closer to the inspired conversation contained in the Text. The problem is the obstacle course that lies between us and the original conversation. We are undoubtedly familiar with some of these obstacles, but others may be foreign.

- **Language.** One of the most obvious obstacles is that of translation and language. People often ask me which translation is "the best" or "the most accurate," but these labels are misnomers. There are always ideas, concepts, and nuances that cannot be translated from one language to another. This makes the work of translation unbelievably complex.

- **Time.** Simply put, a lot changes over the course of two or three thousand years. The assumptions being made back then are radically different from our assumptions now—let alone all the details we've simply lost without realizing it.

- **Culture.** Cultural assumptions have radically changed in our own context over the last few centuries. Imagine how much more that is true for a different culture on a different continent in a different millennium.

- **Literary tools.** We have certain ways of writing in our modern languages. Beyond things like figures of speech and other types of expressions, we have our own familiarities with rhyme and meter. We have emojis and social-media platforms. Most of us pick up on these things in our culture. In the United States, for example, we generally understand the differences between a tweet, a blog post, and an article in the *Wall Street Journal*. We understand the objectives of a newspaper as it compares to an academic journal, a documentary film, or a TikTok video. In the same way, the ancient world of the Bible had a toolbox full of literary devices and approaches that all functioned in unique ways. These are likely the most overlooked and unknown pieces of the interpretive puzzle for the average Bible student.

• **Ever-evolving religious landscape.** The Bible (yes, even the New Testament) was written by Jews into a Jewish context out of different places in Jewish history. But Judaism, just like Christianity or any other faith group, is not an abstract monolith. Judaism evolved throughout history, and Jews grew in their own religious observance and corporate consciousness. The conversations happening during the Exodus were not the conversations happening during the monarchy, which were different than the conversations happening in Persia, which led to the conversations that shaped the rabbinic period—the backdrop of the Gospels and the New Testament letters. Once considered, this observation is obvious, yet the nonacademic Bible teacher rarely explores this reality in depth when engaging in biblical interpretation.

What this means is that we are what Dr. Gary Burge calls "literary tourists":

> We have forgotten that we read the Bible as foreigners, as visitors who have traveled not only to a new geography, but to a new century. We are literary tourists who are deeply in need of a guide.[3]

Too often we come to the Bible without an awareness of our tourism. We think the Bible was written to us, about our current experiences and struggles. We expect it to speak to us directly and in our language. We assume the Bible is assuming the same things we are. We forget Philippians was written by a first-century Jewish rabbi to a small band of believers in a Roman colony who were quite unpopular and worried about their leader, who was sitting in prison. We read about doing all things through Christ who strengthens us (Philippians 4:13), and we convince ourselves that, in fact, we will get that new job as we stick our résumé in the mail.

And while there may be relevant modern application in those events, Paul was not sending a timeless pep talk into the vacuum of history. Paul was writing a very specific message with a specific intended meaning to a specific audience. Remembering that we are not the subject, but literary tourists, is simply good biblical hermeneutics. And it doesn't require a seminary degree to know this and practice this when you read the Bible.

Realizing and accepting our place as literary tourists is a significant part of the journey toward a more faithful engagement with Scripture. We'll find that maintaining this awareness is uncommon and requires some discipline, but it is like anything else—something that can be learned. The confident humility of literary tourism can become the default posture of any student of the Text. We assume there is an endless number of things we are unaware of. Our questions provide the opportunity to dive into discovery and come away with a better awareness of a powerful, inspired conversation happening in the pages of our Bibles.

I have spent my life doubling down on just how good I believe the Bible is, and I've found some amazing tour guides along the way. What they've shown me is that my confidence in the goodness of Scripture was well placed. I believe now more than ever that Jesus was bigger and better than any person ever to live. I believe now more than ever that the Bible is a book unlike any book ever written—inspired and powerful, living and active. And I believe now more than ever that both of those things invite us to lean in and dig deeper.

As I've gone on this journey, I have found, over and over, that my questions and my doubts, rooted in confidence, are actually doorways to deeper discovery and wonder. My faith is more vibrant, and God continues to get bigger and bigger every day.

My invitation is a hopeful one: that you might believe this too. As we move forward into this book, leaning into the exploration of a dynamic and deeper understanding of

Scripture, I pray you will find the same affirmation that I did—from both the scholarship of others and the person of Jesus.

And wherever you come to the Text from—confidence or shaky ground—I can promise you this: When you start asking better questions, you'll find better answers.

RESOURCES REFERENCED

Daring Greatly by Brené Brown
Rising Strong by Brené Brown
A New Kind of Christian by Brian D. McLaren
Interpreting the Gospel of John by Dr. Gary Burge

FOR FURTHER STUDY

How to Read the Bible for All Its Worth by Gordon D.
Fee and Douglas Stuart

CHAPTER 2

PLAYING WITH BOTH HANDS

*The Difference between Eastern
and Western Thinking*

"I want you to imagine that for the last twenty years you've stood at that door." Ray Vander Laan motioned to the large doors at the back of the auditorium. Ray was an expert in biblical context, having studied at Hebrew University and audited rabbinical training at Yeshiva University, and he became one of my most influential teachers in the years that followed. This is the first lesson I can remember hearing from him in person.

"Now, you're not able to enter the room," he continued, "but for twenty years, you've observed it from that particular vantage point. You know the room intimately after years of study. You can tell me all about the dimensions of the stage and the color of the backdrop curtains. What you have seen and know is accurate and true."

"But imagine," Ray said, motioning to the other side of the room, "somebody takes you by the hand and leads you—for the first time—to this side door over here. You're still unable to enter the room yourself, but you are given a brand-new perspective. You notice things you simply couldn't see from that other vantage point. Items that were hiding around a corner and out of view, like that trash can. Now that you are closer to the stage, you see things you couldn't have seen before."

"We have been raised in the modern Western world," he went on to explain, "which means we're taught to see everything a particular way. Each of us has a set of assumptions that we are as unaware of as a fish is of the water it swims in."

"But the Bible," Ray said, "was written *from* a different world and *to* a different world. Its authors weren't writing from a modern Western context; they were writing from an ancient Eastern one. Learning how to think like the people of the Bible is like being taken to a brand-new vantage point for the first time after years of familiarity with the old one."[1]

This lesson opened me up years ago to a whole new set of questions that transformed my life forever, but that was only the beginning of my journey. In the following years, after many more lessons from Ray and others—and multiple trips to Israel, Turkey, Jordan, and the rest of the world of the Bible—I have wondered if my teacher's metaphor went far enough.

It wasn't just that there was "another" perspective out there, as accurate and valuable as my own—something to consider, but not really necessary in the grand scheme of things. The historical world of the Bible seemed to me to be far more critical of a consideration. If we didn't become more aware of these differences (and all the details the original perspective and "vantage point" lacked), we would continue propagating bad readings of the Bible—bad readings that litter the history of Western Christianity and have led to some of the worst tragedies of the last two millennia.

THIS HAND? THAT HAND? WHICH HAND?

Imagine yourself sitting at a piano. When you're playing the piano, the two hands, generally speaking, have different jobs. The left hand plays the bass chords that provide the foundational structure the song is built on. The right hand explores much more of what we would typically call the melody.

So pick a song—any song. (For me, it's Leonard Cohen's "Hallelujah.") Imagine that you—an expert piano player (imagining is fun, isn't it?)—begin to play that song, but only with the left hand. You play the bass chords with confidence and poise, absolutely nailing the delivery.

As perfectly as you played, does anyone in the audience recognize the tune? Chances are, they don't. Unless they are experts or have some insider information, that bass line is just a melody-free set of chords, one likely shared by a few other tunes.

Now let's say you shake your head and reach out your other hand, this time playing the song with your right hand.

Again, perfect delivery. (Well done, by the way.) Does the audience recognize the tune? This time, they clearly do. Of course, they are a little underwhelmed; a few slow claps emerge from the crowd amid the silent confusion.

But not to worry—you're prepared. You jump into a flawless delivery of the song with both hands that brings the audience to their feet, some wiping away tears.

I find this metaphor more fully captures the gravity of reality when it comes to Scripture. If we come to the Bible simply reading it from a Western perspective, asking Western questions and looking for answers that matter to a Western context, it's like playing the song with our left hand. We might nail the delivery and have brilliant chords, but we don't even recognize the song.

If we focus on the Eastern perspective and the questions the ancient world of the Bible was asking, looking for answers that were relevant to the original, inspired conversation, we play the song in the right hand. We recognize the song for what it is and analyze the nuance of the melody.

It's not just "another option" for how to engage the music. It's an unquestionable upgrade from the left-hand-only approach. We are much closer to the beauty of the song and the intent of the Songwriter. But it can still be somewhat cold and detached, a clinical exercise that might stimulate the mind but fails to tickle the soul.

Of course, when we put the two hands together, the song comes to life: the artistic and dramatic delivery impact all who hear it.

SHOW ME THE SHEET MUSIC

Okay, Marty, you might be thinking, *this sounds great. But what do all these metaphors mean? How does this "both hands" thing change how I read the Bible? I need more than abstract ideas and concepts.*

I couldn't agree more. Mental assent to the logic of a thing doesn't get us anywhere—understanding what it really looks like is how we move toward change. So, let's walk through some general ideas to understand what we're dealing with here.

Our Way with Words

The Western mind likes to engage words by using them as tools to describe something more abstract. We gravitate toward definitions. A word, for most of us, is a conduit or a capsule, full of the data that resides in its definition. It's like the cable that carries information between the transmitter and receiver. Because of this, we organize words very systematically, making this information transfer as seamless as possible. We use prose, outlines, and bullet points. Don't believe me? Just look at how we structured what you've read so far, with prose, headings, and subheadings, in a book that is already divided into sections and chapters.

But the Eastern mind sees words as a canvas, not a capsule. A word is a picture, not a pile of data. And a picture, as the saying goes, is worth a thousand words. Biblical Hebrew contains roughly eight thousand words. Modern English has hundreds of thousands. What this means is that while Western languages are built for precision, the Hebrew language packs a lot of depth into every single word.

The Eastern mind sees each word as a picture. Those words are connected to other words in what is often called a "word tree," which is a collection of images that drive the understanding of a word. Because this is how a writer from this context sees words, they prefer poetry and symbolism to outlines and lists.

What's in a number?

For the Westerner, numbers represent, primarily, a quantitative value.

Now, I can imagine you're already thinking, *Uh, yes, Marty. This is just about the only way to understand and describe a number. A number is fundamentally a quantitative value!*

And I certainly wouldn't argue about that from a Western perspective. Remember, the goal of this exercise is not to dismiss our Western perspective or label it wrong, inaccurate, or less "godly." We are instead moving into a healthy recognition that the world of the Bible does not work from the same set of assumptions as the typical Westerner. If I want to understand this inspired conversation, I must understand the assumptions those authors and audiences are working from.

The Easterner sees numbers primarily as qualitative or symbolic. A quick web search on Jewish numerology will reveal everything from deep mysticism and allegorical understandings to deeply systematized relationships with numbers in rabbinic teaching. While the former likely seems a little afield from our conversation, the latter is quite relevant to studying the Bible.

For the Jewish mind, the number five, for example, will immediately evoke an image of the five Books of Moses. If someone from the ancient Jewish context were to see a line of five apples on a table, they would think of Genesis, Exodus, Leviticus, Numbers, and Deuteronomy. Similarly, the number four would bring to mind the four corners of the earth and the pagan nations.

To a Jewish reader, the story of Jesus feeding five thousand in Galilee with five loaves and two fish is full of meaningful numbers. Five represents the Torah, and one thousand is the numerical representation of a people group—so five thousand (5×1000) means "people of the Torah." Two represents the tablets of Moses. Jesus feeds the people of the Torah with the law, and there is enough leftover bread to fill twelve baskets (representing the tribes of Israel).

A true treatment of Eastern numerology would require its own chapter, but in case you are skeptical of this one-paragraph flyby, consider the fact that Jesus later finds himself in the Decapolis, the land of the pagans, and feeds four thousand. Remember that four represents the corners of the Earth, and thereby the pagan nations. This time there are seven baskets left over, representing the seven pagan nations of Canaan from Joshua 3:10.

If the reader is still unconvinced, consider the fact that when Jesus gets in the boat and the disciples start to argue about lunch supplies, Jesus quizzes them about which details in the stories (Mark 8:17-21)? The specific numbers.

Many Westerners may consider numbers boring. But for Eastern thinkers, numbers are a wild adventure.

What's so eternal about life?

When I ask whether you'd be interested in "eternal life," what do you think of? Most Westerners understand eternal life as something detached from this life. Eternity moves in a linear and quantitative fashion, and eternal life starts when this life is over.

For the ancient Easterner, though, eternal life is qualitative. It is a *kind* of life that rings in and throughout every dimension. Eternity always has been and always will be—not because it is linear in nature but because its quality is more transcendent (and more real) than our current physical experience. For the people of the Bible, eternal life was a life lived in harmony with God, and its practical reality was much more rooted in the present than the future. There was a physical participation in something that was "more true" than simply what we see on the surface.

We can even see this difference in the Greek language of the New Testament. There is a word in the Greek for our linear, material experience with life: *bios*, which is the root of English words like *biology*, the study of life. The New Testament writers know how to use this word, but when they talk about eternal life, the authors use the words *aiōnios* and *zóé*, which are both more qualitative terms that express a present-yet-transcendent reality of eternal life.

Putting the "We" Back in "Us"

The Western mind thinks about existence in terms of the individual. In America, our culture fosters an individualism that is unique from the world of the Bible. I grew up in the Pacific Northwest, where I was taught (with pride) about the spirit of "rugged individualism" that made our way of life possible.

This same mentality bled over into our relationship with God. For years, every worship song was about *me* and *I* and *my*. Whether we were singing about "*me* and Jesus" or asking the Lord to "open the eyes of *my* heart," it seemed like our worship experience was like a tunnel with ourselves at one end and God at the other.

Although the church has grown increasingly aware of this tendency in our worship and elsewhere, the reality is that the Western mind primarily focuses on the individual experience. This isn't always a bad thing. Sometimes our personal perspective is helpful for our views of personal responsibility.

The Eastern world of the Bible, however, was oriented and rooted in an understanding of community. Through moments of confession or reflection—times like Yom Kippur (the Day of Atonement)—the ancient Eastern community saw sin as corporate long before the balance shifted to reflecting on it as primarily personal. In the stories of the history of

God's people, writers most often used the pronoun *we*, not *they*. "*We* stood at Mount Sinai." The Lord "brought *us* back from Babylon." The community saw themselves as participants in those ancient stories, not just observers who were detached from history.

The Error of Sin

Most of us with a Western mind understand sin as wrong belief or incorrect thinking, or even the internal impulse that undergirds our sinful behavior. While the sin itself is often an action or behavior, the idea of sin is rooted in what a person knows or desires. We talk about sin as a noun, something inside of us that needs to be expunged. This isn't entirely incorrect from a biblical perspective—a student of the Bible can find plenty of references from both Testaments that speak of sin in this way.

But the Eastern mind more readily identifies sin as wrong behavior, emphasizing what a person does. A friend of mine in Jerusalem, a Jewish shop owner named Moshe, likes to say, "I hear you Christians talk about sin as if it is a blemish that needs to be done away with. Do you want to know how to get rid of sin? Stop doing it!" He says this with a twinkle in his eye and an awareness of the oversimplification, but I appreciate his perspective nonetheless.

Proving God Is

The Western thinker tends to want to prove the existence of God. Many of us are undoubtedly familiar with the Western

Christian apologist, who attempts to use the details of Scripture, partnered with logic or philosophy, to prove that God is undeniably present in the world. The Greek cultural heritage and philosophical bent of the Western world causes us to lean toward the abstract.

The Eastern mind is much more rooted in the concrete—the existence of God is an undeniable source of mystery and all that is unknown. Again, the Western mind has raised many productive and logical conversations, but if we are expecting the ancient Eastern world of the Bible to engage the question of whether God *is*, we will be disappointed. That simply isn't what the authors of the Bible are trying to do.

Who is he anyway?

And now that we've dealt with the existence of God, what does it mean to talk about him? How does each vantage point consider him? You're probably not surprised by the answer: differently.

The Westerner often talks about the nature of God. We use big words to describe abstract truths about God's attributes: omnipresent, omniscient, benevolent, compassionate. Our focus is typically, *What is this God like?*

But the ancient Easterner spoke of God in terms of relationship. Instead of wondering what God is like, they asked, *How does this God relate?* They told stories of their experiences with him. Instead of describing God as omnipotent, they talked about him being a strong tower or a fortress. Instead of saying God is benevolent, they spoke of him as a caring father. Again, we see words operating as images, in contrast to Western terms and definitions.

The Faithfulness of Trust

What is faith? For the Western mind, Christian faith is often something very cerebral, such as the affirmation of a list of beliefs or a creed. Faith is reduced to a list of intellectual assents, which each have their accompanying proof texts to "prove" how biblical each idea is.

Knowing what we believe plays a vital role in faith. But the world of the Bible speaks of faith as something relational. Faith is rooted not in explanations of truth, but rather in a trust that emerges from relationship and past experiences. In fact, in the Eastern mind, trust is a common synonym for faith. Because of this orientation, we rarely see any attempt to rationalize faith in Scripture. Proof texts are hard to find. Faith is an action, inseparable from faithfulness. Faith is what trust looks like in relationship.

The Question of Truth

Pilate asked a famous question that has wriggled its way into many Holy Week homilies. "What is truth?" the flabbergasted Roman governor asked Jesus, trying to figure out why this ragtag rabbi stood in front of him (John 18:38).

For the Westerner—and, indeed, likely even for Pilate himself—truth is rational and scientific. When we talk about truth in Scripture, we often focus on how something was done (consider the way we discuss the "truth" of creation in Genesis 1). Belief in truth, for the Western mind, comes from thinking through the validity of information and ideas.

For the Eastern mind of the Scriptures, truth is less rational and more relational, less scientific and more experiential. When the Easterner looks at truth in Scripture, they focus not on *how* something was done, but on *what* was done and *who* did it. Belief in a truth will come as they experience that truth in concrete ways rather than thinking through abstract realities.

But what about now?

As I sought to understand the ancient Eastern world of the Bible, one of the most helpful concepts was the idea of *truth over time*. Having been raised in a fundamentalist Christian home during the turn of the millennium, I had been routinely warned about the dangers of postmodernity and the culture's ensuing infatuation with what our local prophets called "relative truth."

For the Westerner, truth is an abstract idea that is static and unchanging. Now, before you think I'm about to praise relativism, let me clarify: I'm not. I completely affirm the idea of absolute truth. But in the Western context, we equate absolute truth with our *present understanding* of truth, meaning that we see our current interpretation as static and unchanging. This kind of affirmation of absolute truth creates problems whenever you learn something new—or, maybe more importantly, when you learn you were wrong.

The Eastern mind wouldn't necessarily argue with the concept of absolute truth but understands truth itself to be dynamic. What this means is that *truth continues to unfold over time*. I've come to believe that this actually allows truth to be more absolute: It remains firmly rooted in the same place but dynamically grows and expands as humanity's consciousness, awareness, and collective knowledge grows.

This same truth remains vibrant and alive, even as the world around it changes and adjusts. Rather than being relative, the truth is moving right alongside us, never changing in its absoluteness, but always going to the places God needs it to go to.

YOU DO YOU

Some of you reading this are just soaking all of it up, possibly eager to change your thinking completely to the Eastern mindset. Others of you are really frustrated and concerned about the direction this logic is headed. Am I suggesting that Westerners are deficient and can't understand the Bible? Do we all need to become Eastern in our thinking?

Let's stop and name an important reality: *We cannot change who we are*. Most of my readers are likely Westerners. Try as hard as you like, you cannot make yourself "more Eastern."

And this is okay.

God doesn't need you to become more Eastern. Remember, the song of Scripture is only the beautiful piece that it is when we play it with both hands. In all our wonderful perspectives, we are one of those hands, and we have a part to play. Our perspective gives life and movement to the song. The things we bring to the conversation amplify the truth of Scripture into what we see and understand today.

But it's also important to remember that *our Western perspective* must *acknowledge and interact with the world of the Text*. Our job is to understand the original conversation, inspired by God, between the authors of the Bible and their respective audiences. We need to remember—and seek to understand—that they are working with a different set of assumptions, asking different questions. They have a literary toolbox full of tools we don't have in ours.

This means that as readers, we need to make some adjustments to our own toolbox so that our Bible study is more equipped to have the right conversation. As we journey through the rest of this book, you get to pick up the tools that resonate with you the most and ask the questions that allow you to become more fluent in the ancient conversation of the biblical world.

Each of the topics we've touched on in this chapter alone could easily be expanded as we grapple with implications and nuances. Although I have some definite thoughts about each of these, such an examination would likely drift outside my expertise and play dangerously in the realm of opinion and projection. Besides, our goals here are different. *We're striving to form a new and deeper way of thinking about Scripture.* This is the beginning of your journey, the sketched-out map for the road ahead, not the destination.

In the chapters ahead, we're going to look at all the different portions of Scripture, examining how they are unique in structure and intent. If we can see the different parts of the Bible for what they are—instead of just treating the Bible as a big book that reads the same from cover to cover—then we can start appreciating each aspect. When we realize that we get to spend our lives exploring the nuances and pieces of Scripture, we no longer have to be intimidated by the impossible task of mastery, or "knowing our Bibles."

At the end of each chapter, you'll find a list of resources that directly shaped the things I shared in that chapter, as well as a list of resources for further study and consideration. These resources will range from the deeply academic to the more accessible, but they are designed to help others pursue their own journey at their own pace. The goal is to help you experiment with new tools and examine the ones that you're used to.

Remember, if all we do is blast the subwoofer with a strong bass line, we aren't playing actual music. We're just annoying the neighbors. Let's learn instead how to play with both hands. The song is too beautiful, too moving, too powerful to not learn all the notes.

RESOURCES REFERENCED

For another tour of the same information, listen to episode 0 of *The BEMA Podcast*[2]: http://www.BEMAdiscipleship.com/0

Numerical Secrets of the Bible by Casper J. Labuschagne
The Heart of a People by Moshe Avraham Kempinski
The Gifts of the Jews by Thomas Cahill
Abraham by Bruce Feiler

FOR FURTHER STUDY

Misreading Scripture with Western Eyes by E. Randolph
   Richards and Brandon J. O'Brien
The Epic of Eden by Sandra L. Richter
Sitting at the Feet of Rabbi Jesus by Ann Spangler and
   Lois Tverberg
The Forgotten Jesus by Robby Gallaty
Inspired by Rachel Held Evans
Our Father Abraham by Marvin R. Wilson

CHAPTER 3

LETTING TORAH READ YOU

Looking for Literary Devices

"I simply don't have the time or the money for this!" I said, frustrated. The current season was financially and emotionally tight, and my wife had just informed me that the garbage disposal had completely seized up. I was out of patience. How could I possibly handle this?

It wasn't the first time that week I'd been faced with this kind of dilemma. Just days before, a taillight bulb burned out on my truck—right after I'd brought it home from the auto shop. But fortunately, in that situation, I'd learned something new.

As a campus minister, I often find myself surrounded by college students. I had been lamenting about having to schedule another expensive appointment for my car when one of them said, "Why don't you replace the bulb yourself?"

"You don't understand," I said. "I used to work on cars when I was younger, but I always relied on my dad to help me. I wouldn't even know where to begin. And the moment that I tear into one thing, I will likely damage something else. Nope. The only option is to take it back to the shop."

The student shook his head, unimpressed. "You've heard of this thing called YouTube?"

Immediately, I felt like an idiot. I had watched college students do this kind of thing and lauded them for it. I talk about it frequently when I travel and speak about campus ministry. Why had I never considered this opportunity as accessible to me?

That afternoon, I purchased a replacement bulb and headed home. I did a quick search for "replacing taillight bulb on 1996 Chevy pickup," found a seven-minute how-to video, and in less than eighteen minutes (I'm a slow worker), I had successfully fixed my problem. It cost me just over two dollars.

The tool was there the whole time. I just needed somebody to tell me about it—and everything changed.

It took me a second, but as I stood at my kitchen sink thinking about the garbage disposal, I remembered my new method. Sure enough, a few minutes later I had found a video and a remedy to our problem.

This experience has repeated itself again and again. I

don't want to be overly dramatic, but it has—on a very practical level—changed my life. Learning about tools and resources can do that. When somebody tells you where to look and what to look for, a whole world is opened to you. And that holds particularly true for a part of the Scripture many of us don't wholly know what to do with: the Torah.

THOSE BOOKS ARE DIFFERENT

The Western world, built for efficacy and efficiency, opts for a direct and streamlined teaching approach. We build sermons, presentations, and blog posts around systematic reasoning. Using inductive or deductive reasoning, the Western mind wants to pass a proposition or set of data on to the learner. The information is presented to maximize consumption and retention (who doesn't love a four-part presentation with alliterated points?) with as little hindrance as possible.

The Eastern world believes that a unique kind of learning happens if the teacher takes a completely different approach. When learning becomes an act of discovery, it becomes, to the Eastern mind, much more intimate and complete. The impact of the words increases exponentially when the writer tells a story or gives an instruction with layers and levels of meaning. And the student who is willing to do the work is rewarded with ever-expanding insight.

The typical Jewish story or teaching has an obvious

moral that can be uncovered with a straightforward exegesis. If we're keeping in mind all the contextual details we've discussed, a plain reading of the Text has much to offer. But while the surface-level reading is not wasted effort, we should not miss the opportunity to discover layer upon layer of additional meaning—treasure buried in the Text. The additional layers will never change the meaning of what we see on the surface, but they will expand on it, adding color to the original understanding or addressing added complexity in its application.

Why is this important as we approach the Torah? Because the Torah is central to Jews' understanding of who God is and what humans are called to do and be. The whole Tanakh (the Hebrew Scriptures, which many of us call the "Old Testament"—more on this later) is inspired and authoritative, but in the Jewish mind, each part of the Tanakh has a differing priority of authority. At the risk of oversimplifying a complex conversation, the Books of Moses, known as the Torah, carry the primary authority of the Hebrew Scriptures.

It's vital we understand this because our Bible is a Jewish work, written to and from a Jewish world, working with Jewish assumptions. When Jesus, a Jewish rabbi, engages in religious discourse, he makes "legal" arguments that follow these assumptions. To put it another way, he "plays by the rules" of Jewish understanding. The apostle Paul does the same thing in his writings. (Again, we'll address this more in later chapters.)

So, when we are in the Torah, how do we ask better questions? How do we learn to ask the questions the author and audience of the Torah were asking?

Here's your first key for reading the Torah: *Watch how literary devices are used.* What kinds of literary devices can we be looking for? Some examples are

- chiasmus,
- borrowed culture narrative,
- historical subtext,
- parallelism, and
- borrowed literary genre.

Let's look at some of these and how they function. As we do, remember that the goal of an Eastern author or teacher is to bury treasure in a teaching or story. They are adding multiple layers of depth into the story intentionally, which increases the amount of discovery and payoff for the invested student of the Torah.

Chiasmus

A chiasm is one of the most objective and deliberate literary tools one can find in the Torah. As I use the term here, I am typically referring to what is known as "inverted parallelism."[1]

A chiasm is a very effective way for an author to bury

a treasure within a story. The story is constructed in an inverted fashion with distinct parts or phrasing. The first part of the story mirrors the last part, the second part of the story mirrors the second to the last part, and so on, until the story works itself toward the center of the chiasm. It is here where the audience finds buried treasure.

One of my favorite teachers is Rabbi David Fohrman, who engages in this kind of textual interpretation well. While he and I diverge in our beliefs about Jesus, I firmly believe that watching an Orthodox Jewish teacher like Fohrman provides invaluable insight into how the Eastern biblical mind constructed the biblical text.[2]

I have learned from Rabbi Fohrman that we can observe these chiasms at work all throughout the Torah. Much of Jewish interpretation suggests that all the stories of Genesis 1–11 are chiasms and that together, they potentially even form a larger chiastic unit.

One example of a chiasmus is the account of God instituting circumcision in Genesis 17. If we move beyond the surface reading of the story, which itself is loaded with meaning, we might notice that the story begins and ends with a discussion about covenants (verse 2 is A1 and verse 19 is A2). If we move one layer toward the center, we see Abram falling facedown (verse 3 is B1 and verse 17 is B2). Take another step toward the center, and we have name changes—Abram's in verse 5 (C1) and Sarai's in verse 15 (C2). Finally, we read mentions of everlasting covenants in verses 7 (D1) and 13 (D2).

CHIASM EXAMPLE 1

A1 covenant (*Genesis 17:2*)

    B1 Abram falls facedown (*Genesis 17:3*)

        C1 Abram's name change (*Genesis 17:5*)

            D1 everlasting covenant (*Genesis 17:7*)

                CENTER every male to be circumcised (community free of hierarchy; *Genesis 17:9-12*)

            D2 everlasting covenant (*Genesis 17:13*)

        C2 Sarai's name change (*Genesis 17:15*)

    B2 Abraham falls facedown (*Genesis 17:17*)

A2 covenant (*Genesis 17:19*)[3]

All this leads to a buried treasure at the center of the story: Every male, every last one of them, would be circumcised. When you examine this center in relationship to the layers of the chiasm, a new layer of complexity begins to form. God is inviting the family of God to be a community free of distinction and hierarchy. No longer is Abram an "exalted father"; he is simply Abraham, "father of many." No longer is Sarai "my princess"—her identity shifts from being anyone's possession to "princess."

This buried treasure expands on the surface-level reading with layers of color and complexity, adding richness and interpretive depth to the story.

Another account that provides a straightforward chiasm is that of Noah. It's easy to see this chiasm because of its use of numbers. If you find the number seven and then another seven and then forty and then one hundred and fifty, you will notice that the numbers reverse on the back side of the story—one hundred and fifty, then forty, then seven, and finally seven. This helps you clearly identify the center as Genesis 8:1: God remembering Noah while he's in the ark. But why is that the center treasure?

CHIASM EXAMPLE 2

A1 seven days (*Genesis 7:4*)

   B1 seven days (*Genesis 7:10*)

      C1 forty days (*Genesis 7:17*)

         D1 a hundred and fifty days (*Genesis 7:24*)

            CENTER "God remembered . . . waters receded . . . rain had stopped" (*Genesis 8:1-2*)

         D2 a hundred and fifty days (*Genesis 8:3*)

      C2 forty days (*Genesis 8:6*)

   B2 seven days (*Genesis 8:10*)

A2 seven days (*Genesis 8:12*)

For this, we look to our next literary device.

Borrowed Cultural Narrative

Long before Genesis was penned, flood narratives were plentiful in almost every culture of the ancient Near East. Much of my Bible education tried to use apologetics to prove that Genesis was the first. I believe this focus was foolhardy. Not only does almost all historical scholarship disagree with this assessment, but insisting that this flood narrative came first robs the story of much of its inspired brilliance.

Flood narratives were present in Sumerian literature, the world of Chaldea and Mesopotamia, Egyptian lore, and other places in almost every direction.[4] *The Epic of Gilgamesh* is one famous variation of this dominant cultural narrative in the ancient Eastern world. What is so striking about the flood narrative found in Genesis is how it differs from the cultural norm.

Every flood narrative started the same way. The world is corrupted and polluted with human mischief, foolishness, and impurity. The gods (whether one in particular or many in tandem) gather to purify the world, bathing it in a great deluge, sometimes locally and sometimes globally. In *The Epic of Gilgamesh*, some of the characters are on a quest to interact with these gods. At one point, one of the main characters, Utnapishtim, is told by the god Enkidu to build a raft through which he will save all life—the life of his family and the animals. The parallels to the story of the Genesis flood are striking, and we can quickly see why my Bible college treated it as a threat to biblical truth.

But *The Epic of Gilgamesh* represents what is true in almost all ancient flood narratives. The gods are in conflict, their anger is threatening the safety of creation, and humankind must respond appropriately to outsmart or appease these deities. It's almost always a story of humans against the gods.

But the story in Genesis is astonishingly different. While it starts in the same fashion—the corruption of mankind and a God desiring to "wash creation" and restore its goodness—the story quickly takes a unique turn: The very God seeking to purge the earth is simultaneously scheming to save it. Not only this, but it is God who arranges the divine partnership and leads Noah to success. In other words, the internal details of the story lack logical consistency. The author must be trying to pull the reader into some other point, knocking them off-balance from their normal expectations.

As the story begins with God lamenting "every inclination of the thoughts of the human heart was only evil all the time" (Genesis 6:5), it ends (remember the chiasm?) with a similar-yet-altered statement: *Even though* every inclination of the human heart is evil, God will never again flood the earth (Genesis 8:21). This is a stark contrast to other flood narratives, which leave the reader with a sense of uncertainty. This God of the Bible promises not to be like the gods of the people's cultural folklore. He even promises not to do this *even though* things get that corrupted again. What kind of a crazy story is this? What kind of accountability exists if God promises never again to destroy the earth? Isn't fear the one card God has to play here? Why is he giving that up?

And it is in this observation that we find the brilliance of what Genesis is doing. By employing these literary devices, it is telling us a story underneath the stories: *This God is not like the gods you are used to. This God is wildly different.*

Yet most of us miss this point of the story entirely as we argue about the historicity of an ancient global flood. It's a perfect example of asking questions the Bible isn't asking and always getting the wrong answer. We fail to find the buried treasure the story is trying to teach us.

But what did any of this have to do with Genesis 8:1 and God remembering Noah? Oh yes, thank you for remembering. Let's move on to the next literary device.

Historical Subtext

Some of you may see this heading and assume we're just talking about historical context. But while historical subtext is very closely related to that, what we are discussing here is how certain literary approaches are built on historical structures.

In her fantastic book *The Epic of Eden*, Sandra Richter speaks to the historical context of covenants in the ancient Near East. One of the most common covenants we encounter throughout ancient Eastern history is the suzerain-vassal covenant. These covenants are constructed around the idea that there is a greater, much more dominant party, known as the suzerain. The suzerain is typically an imperial power subjugating its neighbors into a forced alliance. These lesser parties are known as vassals. They are forced into these arrangements, where they pay tributes (i.e., taxes) to the suzerain and promise their political support and allegiance;

in return, they get the imperial protection of the suzerain for being part of their empire.

This relationship is tenuous at best, built on shaky ground. As a vassal, you have virtually no leverage, you are responsible for producing all the "receipts" of said agreements when needed, and it's doubtful whether those agreements will be honored.

It should come as no surprise that in all the covenant relationships between God and his people, God is the Suzerain. In the story of Noah, Noah is unquestionably the vassal. Yet it is God who "keeps the receipts" for his covenant agreement. It is the Suzerain who "remembers" Noah in the ark. It is the Suzerain who takes his threat of power and retaliation, his "bow" (the Hebrew word for rainbow is simply the word for *bow*, a weapon of war and judgment), and puts it in the clouds, pointed up so that he—the Suzerain—will always remember the agreement.

To top it off, God promises never to destroy the earth again with a flood. What kind of suzerain-vassal nonsense is this? What kind of a God is this? What leverage does a suzerain have if he doesn't have the threat of vengeance and the ability to hold his vassal captive in fear?

No matter how you slice and dice your literary devices, when you start asking the questions the Bible is asking, you start getting the right answers. And might I add, these answers start to look an awful lot like Jesus and sound an awful lot like the gospel. What's so stunning is that we got here using Jewish hermeneutics and noticing literary devices from their ancient playbook rather than using Western systematic theology, which has consistently led us to much different, less Jesus-y answers. This is the power of asking better questions.

Parallelism

Have you ever noticed how sometimes there is just something funny about the chronology of the larger narrative in the Torah? Sometimes there's nothing technically wrong or "off," but you just can't shake the way the imagery flows in your head.

Let's head over to Genesis 21 to see an example of this. The chapter starts with the birth of Isaac. In the next section, we learn about Isaac being weaned and Ishmael "mocking" Isaac, which tragically leads to Hagar and Ishmael being expelled from the household. As they run out of water and provisions in the desert, Hagar takes her son and lays him under a nearby bush. She then walks away and prepares for his death.

Now, what image do you have of the boy being laid under the bush? I find most of us picture a baby or an infant. But Ishmael is at least fifteen years old.[5] It's difficult to imagine a young, sturdy child being in worse shape than his more aged mother, yet here we are. The whole thing makes you feel like the story is awkwardly out of place in the narrative. The chapter ends with a treaty and covenant at Beersheba.

So now let's move to the next chapter. God asks Abraham to take Isaac and sacrifice him on a mountain. Notice how many parallels there are between these two chapters:

SIMILAR IMAGERY IN GENESIS CHAPTERS 21 AND 22

Genesis 21	Genesis 22
The phrase "early the next morning" is present (verse 14).	The phrase "early the next morning" is present (verse 3).
Abraham sets supplies on Hagar's shoulders (verse 14).	Abraham sets supplies on Isaac's shoulders (verse 6).
Hagar puts the boy under the "wood" (verse 15).	Abraham puts the boy on the wood (verse 9).
Hagar, needing water, looks up to see a well (verse 19).	Abraham, needing a sacrificial animal, looks up to see a ram (verse 13).
The story ends with a covenant (verses 27-31).	The story ends with a covenant (verses 15-18).

These stories contain the same phrasing and elements in the same order!

My point? These stories are, without question, parallel stories that are intentionally juxtaposed. This is deliberate parallelism. If one continues to examine the story, they will find out that the story of the *Akedah* (the binding of Isaac) is, in fact, another chiasm with a treasure buried at its center.[6] These two stories juxtapose the idea of faithfulness. The defining characteristic of God's family is a commitment to not leave each other's sides, even in the most trying of circumstances.

Borrowed Literary Forms

Sometimes the Bible deliberately plays on a literary genre that was well known in its day. You see this with the creation narratives and stories of origins in Genesis 1–11. Creation myth was a familiar cultural genre in the time Genesis was written. Even though it lands outside the scope of the Torah, the book of Joshua follows the exact script (with, just like the Genesis stories, striking distinctions) of what many call a "conquest narrative" genre, which we find all throughout Hittite, Egyptian, and even Assyrian cultures.[7]

A great example of this is found in the book of Deuteronomy. Remember our earlier discussion about suzerain-vassal covenants? We have enough of them on record that some scholars have identified a consistent format—and if we look at how Deuteronomy (and, to some extent, Leviticus) unfolds, we'll notice that it follows this outline almost perfectly:

Preamble: The covenant gives some opening statements for the record.

History: The covenant outlines the story that brought the parties to this place, usually emphasizing the greatness of the suzerain and exaggerating the pathetic nature of the vassal.

Rules: Stipulations of the covenants are outlined, rules to be followed are laid out, and other terms of the agreement are established.

Rewards and punishments: If you follow the rules, things will go well; if you don't follow the rules, things will be bad—really bad. This section almost always overdoes the warnings of just what the suzerain will do if they are betrayed.

Summary: The covenant is summarized, usually in the form of a song that can be sung and repeated (since most members of the party do not get a copy).[8]

We can debate whether Deuteronomy has a preamble, but everything else is there: a history (chapters 1–3), a set of rules (chapters 4–26), a description of rewards and punishments that is weighted toward the warnings (27–30), and the song of Moses to close (chapter 32).

Some scholars have even noted that the five books of the Torah fit this model as well. Genesis serves as the preamble, Exodus as the historical narrative, Leviticus as the stipulations, Numbers as a record of rewards and punishments (heavy on the latter), and Deuteronomy as the song.

———

I know—that's a lot. What we just discussed probably raises about a hundred new questions for many of you, and all this context feels a little overwhelming. But those questions are good. They are the beginning stages of noticing *the conversation that the Bible is having*. Mainly, what we are trying to do is realize with new clarity the intentions behind the Torah—what was understood by the original audience and intended by the author. This was a very large part of the inspired conversation.

The Torah is a gigantic treasure hunt packed full of meaning—and this shouldn't surprise us. For the Jewish audience, this is the teaching of Moses! This is where their covenant relationship with God began, through the teaching of the greatest Jewish teacher, the man who knew God personally and spoke with him face to face (Deuteronomy 34:10-12).

The rest of the Tanakh is an expanding, inspired, continued reflection on the teaching found in the Torah. It is the story of God's people as they lived into this covenant relationship. So we would expect that, more than any other place in the Tanakh, the Torah will be where all the complexity, beauty, depth, and treasure hunts begin.

We exegete the Scriptures just like we always have. But we must realize that this exegesis only partly involves interacting with surface-level conversations. We need to avoid the Western temptation to look outside and start talking apologetics, asking questions the Bible isn't asking—and we need to learn to start going further *inside* the Text to find out what kinds of literary tools might add color and depth to our understanding of these stories and passages.

A WORD ABOUT PROBLEMS

Did you notice how many of these literary devices are found when you start paying attention to "problems" in the Text? We find the chiasm by noticing the awkward repetition. We find the historical subtext by asking why Deuteronomy includes all the gruesome details of reward and punishment.

We find the parallelism by acknowledging that the chronology seems a little off.

Our Western sensibilities have hamstrung our ability to ask the right questions in part because we've spent so much time trying to prove how right and how accurate and how historical the Bible is. But the Bible isn't trying to validate itself; the Bible is trying to transform its reader.

I am routinely told by listeners of our podcast that one of the most helpful and freeing things they've learned is how to pay attention to the problems. It takes a lot of reprogramming, but once they manage to do so, everything changes in how they engage the Bible and interact with buried treasure. Instead of seeing problems as things that need to be resolved and explained so they can get back to "trusting the Bible," they see those problems as lights that go off on their mental dashboard, inviting them to pull over and start doing some digging.

A talking snake? Folks, that's not normal. There's probably some buried treasure there. Don't run past that.

A woman mentioned in a genealogy? That's quite strange in ancient Jewish genealogical records from a male-oriented society. Slow down and start paying attention to why she is there.

When you start to feel uncomfortable about the God you're encountering, don't ignore that—when we harbor that stuff inside, it comes out in some of the unhealthiest of ways. Instead, lean in and see if it's actually the beginning of a treasure map.

A WHAT-RASH?

Now you may be wondering: *How do we know we're seeing the right problems in the Torah (or elsewhere)? How do we know if we're asking the right questions?*

Well, luckily, there's a group of people, known as the Jews, who have been working with the Torah a lot longer than we Christians have. They understand the context and the literary tools. They've had the best of the best thinkers and teachers working on this project for some time. So one of the best places I like to go to learn is the Jewish tradition. It's a giant, collected historical commentary.

For Orthodox Jews, this historical commentary is also authoritative—inspired on some level and part of the canon. Part of this is what they call *halakhah*, the authorized understanding of how to interpret and live out the Scriptures. Other pieces are more like a collection of commentaries and stories. Some of it is ancient and some of it is medieval, and some can even be more modern. Some of the ancient portions, like the Mishnah, can be relevant to us as Jesus followers because they shed light on the way the world of Jesus thought back in the Second Temple period.

For myself—and most of you reading, I imagine—I don't find this library to be inspired and authoritative. It does not carry the same weight as written Scripture. I believe, however, that it is one of the best commentaries for interpreting the Torah.

So how do we use this commentary? We ask, *What have*

some of those ancient sages and rabbis seen when they looked at the Text? and intentionally avoid drawing major conclusions that a few thousand years of rabbis haven't found. When checking ancient (or modern) opinions, we hold them against the teaching and life of Jesus and ask, *Does this match up?* If it doesn't look like Jesus, then it doesn't make the cut as a possible interpretation. But, as you'll notice in some of the examples we used in this chapter, many of these interpretations look *more* like Jesus than the "Christian" and Western interpretations we're used to.

Many of these references and stories will be referred to as *midrash. Midrash* can be a confusing term. Used in a very general sense, it can mean telling an interpretive story. For instance, I could tell a midrash about Jesus' teaching on loving your enemies, and there'd be no authority to it, since it's merely a story I tell. *Midrash* can also refer to any ancient story or interpretation told in Jewish tradition ("There's a midrash about Abraham and a fiery furnace . . .").

Then there is *midrash* used in the sense of *the* Midrash, with a capital *M*. This section of the Jewish oral tradition is canonized as part of sacred Jewish literature and is considered official Jewish interpretation.[9]

I say all this because the midrash offers us a great way of checking our treasures against the literary treasury of those who have worked with this book for centuries longer than Christian thinkers have. There is absolutely no guarantee that they are right, and I would say that there are times they are wrong, but so it is with any commentary I pull off my shelf.

This ancient Jewish library shows itself even more credible for us as Christians because some of the ancient portions are referenced throughout the New Testament. The midrash was a reality for the New Testament authors as they engaged the Text—from some of Jesus' teachings in the Gospels to direct references from Paul and the author of Hebrews to the book of Jude (which is practically half midrash in what it references).

A DYNAMIC TORAH

Often we treat the Torah as a static record of history rather than something dynamic that leads us to buried treasure. The Jews have understood the dynamic potential of the Torah for some time. They have a practice when learning the Talmud[10] that I have found instructive. Ilana Kurshan makes some fascinating observations on this practice in her book *If All the Seas Were Ink*:

> When completing a tractate of Talmud, it is customary to recite a prayer known as the *hadran*: *hadran alach v'hadrach alan*. Hadran comes from the word for return, though in modern Hebrew it is used to refer to an encore. This is one way the rabbis use the term, suggesting that the text continues to go on even after we have finished it, since there is always more to learn. According to this understanding, the prayer means "may we return to you, and may you

return to us": May we have the opportunity to study this tractate again (because inevitably we'll forget some of what we learn), and may it come back to us (because we hope that some of what we learn will stay with us). The prayer gives voice to my fervent belief in the power of learning to make the world endlessly interesting—there is always more to learn, which means that there is always a reason to keep living. But in classic Talmudic wordplay, hadran, from the word *hadar*, also means "beauty" and "glory." So the prayer can also mean, "Our beauty is from you, and your beauty is from us," which conveys the notion that we, with our own individual life experiences and our own unique perspectives, can beautify the study of Talmud; and Talmud can beautify us.[11]

Now, Kurshan's quote speaks specifically to the Talmud. But the study of the Talmud, in the Jewish mind, is the study of the Torah, so the principle holds true. The beauty of the learning process, the treasure hunts, and the discovery is a continual beautification project, dynamic and lovely.

These treasure hunts aren't abstract realities that happen in a vacuum. They are dynamic relationships that find their beauty and fulfillment only in the engagement and experience of God's people. It's like planning the most amazing birthday party for your friend: The magic isn't in the planning but in the experience.

When God's people engage in these dynamic, living-and-active treasure hunts, Scripture comes to life with a new kind of beauty. We quit looking at the ancient Texts from the cold distance of history and instead lean in with a sense of wonder and curiosity. We begin to believe that God's inspired words have the power to speak messages to us every day—even this one—and that is when the Torah begins to read us.

And so, as we study the Torah,

May we return to you,
    and may you return to us.
For our beauty is from you,
    and your beauty is from us.

RESOURCES REFERENCED

Poet & Peasant / Through Peasant Eyes by Kenneth E. Bailey

endless lessons at Aleph Beta Academy (alephbeta.org) from Rabbi David Fohrman and his team[12]

Episodes 1–7 of *The BEMA Podcast* explore the chiasms of Genesis 1–11 in more depth.

The Epic of Eden by Sandra L. Richter

"A Covenant Guarantee" by Ray Vander Laan: https://www.thattheworldmayknow.com/a-covenant -guarantee

the Jewish virtual library at Sefaria.org

If All the Seas Were Ink by Ilana Kurshan

FOR FURTHER STUDY

The Lost World of Genesis One by John H. Walton

The Lost World of Adam and Eve by John H. Walton

The Evolution of Adam by Peter Enns

The Lost World of the Flood by Tremper Longman III and John H. Walton

Genesis: A Parsha Companion and *Exodus: A Parsha Companion* by Rabbi David Fohrman.

The Exodus You Almost Passed Over by Rabbi David Fohrman

The Beast that Crouches at the Door by Rabbi David Fohrman

CHAPTER 4

HISTORY
AS PROPHECY

History Has an Agenda

The neighbors called the cops.

It was a friend's birthday party. We sat outside around a bonfire late on a cool autumn night, having a raucous (apparently too raucous) debate around a topic of the utmost importance.

What is the correct order to watch the Star Wars movies? When our young children get to watch the series, which episodes will they start with?

Nothing gets a bunch of nerdy young adults fired up like discussing fantasy entertainment. (My opinion, of course, is the correct one. You watch the Star Wars movies in the order of their release.)

The conversation began to get animated as the group discussed the legitimacy of the prequels. I love to be the antagonist in times like these, so the group was already spitting frustration at my suggestion that Jar Jar Binks was a good addition to the franchise. Some people were fuming. (Apparently the neighbors were as well.)

I also decided to suggest that the movies could be watched in linear order. Art can speak to us in different ways, and so it was foolishness, I argued, to believe that there was one singular way to experience the content. We should allow our children the benefit of experiencing the movies in a way we never got to.

Of course, I don't believe that argument for a second. (What kind of Star Wars fan do you think I am?) It was just fun to watch people throw their drinks and yell at the top of their lungs. (I'd like to say I was joking, but remember the part about calling the cops?)

Before I felt God pushing me into ministry, I had dreams of becoming an attorney. I like to think that there's a latent legal prowess inside me that takes joy in successfully making a ridiculous argument when the stakes are low and entertaining.

Now, why is my argument so ridiculous? Because one of the greatest reveals and plot twists of cinematic history—the climactic scene where the hero discovers that the villain is his father—happens in the original episodes. If you watch the movies in linear order rather than order of release, then you would know the plot twist ahead of time. It would radically change the way the story unfolds and how you experience the narrative.

CHRISTIAN CANON REORDERS THE EXPERIENCE

And yet, this kind of reordering is precisely what early Christian leaders did with the biblical canon that we use every day.

I've mentioned the Tanakh a few times and referenced it as the Hebrew Scriptures, the part of the Bible that most Christians know as the Old Testament. The contents of the Tanakh, book by book, are the same as the Old Testament found in a Christian Bible—but the Christian canon significantly rearranged the order of those books.

Why did Christians rearrange the Hebrew Scriptures for the Christian Bible? There's a lot of debate around the motivations. Some argue vehemently that it was simply about reorganizing a relatively new canon (Judaism itself formalized its canon not long before) in what seemed like a more logical, historical, and categorical way. The Christian canon starts with the Books of Moses, followed by historical books, followed by wisdom literature, and closing with "major" and then "minor" prophets. Much of this makes sense and seems harmless enough.

The more cynical observer might see the potential for this order, especially at that particular point in history, to have been driven by intentional anti-Semitism. The Tanakh was designed to end with the record of 2 Chronicles, which means that the final word in the Jewish Scriptures is a declaration of hope and a promise that God will restore them to their land. The Christian rearrangement conveniently shuffles that book to the middle of the Old Testament, before all the warning and condemnation from the prophets, before ultimately ending the testament with Malachi, whose closing words are a curse pointed at a rejection of (what could be) the Messiah.

No matter how we see the motivation, the results of this reordering are significant and worth examining. So let's start with how the Hebrew Scriptures were arranged—the "Bible," if you will, of Jesus and the New Testament authors, before we rearranged it. While this canon was not yet finalized at the time—and nobody in the first century was walking around with a codex form of their Scriptures—the categorical arrangement will be instructive nonetheless.

Tanakh is a shorthand expression (common for Hebrew) that combines the leading consonants of multiple words into a combined expression (almost like an acronym). Some express this by capitalizing the consonants as follows: TaNaKh. The emphasis on the letters *T*, *N*, and *K* points to the three major bodies of the Hebrew Scriptures: Torah, Nevi'im, and Ketuvim.

The Torah is easy enough. We are familiar with the Pentateuch, or the Books of Moses, and the Jewish arrangement offers no surprising curve balls:

TORAH
Genesis
Exodus
Leviticus
Numbers
Deuteronomy

The Nevi'im are the Prophets. At first glance, this might seem insignificant. *Okay, so they put their prophets after the Books of Moses. No big deal.* But upon closer inspection, both the contents of the Nevi'im and the arrangement are unexpected for the average Christian Bible student:

NEVI'IM

The Former Prophets
Joshua
Judges
Samuel
Kings

The Latter Prophets
Isaiah
Jeremiah
Ezekiel

The Twelve
Hosea
Joel

Amos

Obadiah

Jonah

Micah

Nahum

Habakkuk

Zephaniah

Haggai

Zechariah

Malachi

What strikes you as different about that? Make a mental note. Before we dig into what we're seeing here, we'll finish our survey of the Tanakh.

The Ketuvim are the Writings. This was the last part of the Tanakh to be canonized—the process was still taking place during the days of Jesus. Second Temple Judaism was very familiar with "the law and the prophets," referencing the Torah and Nevi'im, and they had all the pieces to the Ketuvim. But they were still deciding what exactly to do with those pieces—how to order them, incorporate them into synagogue, and treat them as a part of the canon. In the strictest sense of the idea, Jewish tradition never truly finalized the book order of the Ketuvim. The Babylonian Talmud had a different order than the other codices. These latter codices have the Ketuvim closing with Ezra/Nehemiah, so our ongoing discussion assumes the more popular Babylonian arrangement, which you will find in almost any Jewish Tanakh today.

KETUVIM

The Poetic Books
Psalms

Proverbs

Job

The Five Scrolls
Song of Songs

Ruth

Lamentations

Ecclesiastes

Esther

Other Books
Daniel

Ezra/Nehemiah

Chronicles

Some of us might not be too thrown by the general outline of the Jewish canon—Torah, Prophets (Nevi'im), and Writings (Ketuvim). But remember—right now we're talking about what we would call the "history" portion of the Old Testament. The Jewish canon has no such section.

Okay, you might say, *it's not a big deal to simply shuffle those history books into the Ketuvim.* But in fact, while some "history" books end up there (Ruth, Esther, Ezra/Nehemiah, Chronicles), the rest of them do not. It's also worth noting that some "prophets"—including Daniel, one of the most "prophetic" books in the Christian mind—end up in the Ketuvim as well!

Now, we could spend a whole book talking about this whole canon order, but here we're going to return to the Nevi'im and ask some questions about what we see. What does this difference between the Christian canon and the Jewish canon have to do with how we read the history of the Tanakh?

SO WHAT?

Let's just pause for a moment and look back at "The Former Prophets" of the Nevi'im. There's a significant difference from what we're used to, right? Joshua is a *prophet*? Judges as well? Samuel and Kings seem like some of the most straightforward history in the Bible, but these are former prophets too?

Part of our confusion emerges from how the Western mind sees history. Westerners see the "job" of history in journalistic ways. Give me the truth, the whole truth, and nothing but the truth. Report on the facts, and do everything you can to avoid bias. The point of recording history is, for us, accuracy.

But the Eastern mind isn't as concerned with that list of priorities. In the world of the Bible, writing things down was a big deal, requiring a lot of time, expertise, and resources. There was no printing press, copy machine, or email—and nothing nearly as easy as pounding away on a computer and saving something to the cloud. You'd have to hire a scribe (or be one) and find the materials to record historical accounts. Such an undertaking needed to do more than simply provide a record.

Just as we learned with the Torah (chapter 3), the Eastern thinker wants to bury meaning and provoke discovery. They believe they are writing about history for a purpose greater than pure accuracy. They are writing for transformation. The thought being, *If we're going to take all this time to write down, read about, and consider history, our goal is that we will be stirred, provoked, and changed.*

History, in the Eastern mind, should make us different people. And in this way, the work of history is *prophetic.*

When I use terms like *prophet* or *prophetic*, I don't mean them in a future-telling sense. Many Christians associate the word *prophecy* with the idea that somebody has been given special access to God's "crystal ball" and a message about where all this is headed. While we can't overcorrect and say that this is absent from the work of prophecy, we would do ourselves a major favor if we largely unhitch these concepts from each other.

To be a prophet is to have something helpful to say. It is to be a mouthpiece for God. It is, as Abraham Joshua Heschel said, to share in the *pathos* of God and share that experience with God's people.[1]

So the Hebrew historians are prophets. They have seen the story of God's people, and they have seen it through the eyes of God. They have shared in some experience with the Creator, and they desire to tell the story of God's people in a way that helps them see it the way God does.

In other words, the Hebrew historian is a prophet with an agenda. The Hebrew historian absolutely has a bias—a God bias, an inspired bias. They are not trying to render an abstract, impartial, fully accurate account of history. Instead, they are trying to tell the story of God's people in a way that illuminates what God is doing in their midst and what he is inviting them to become. Their emphasis is on the spiritual formation of God's people.

Now, we may not like this approach to history. We may have a difficult time unhitching the concept of Western journalism from ancient Eastern history. But this is where we will be confronted with the importance of asking the questions the Bible is asking. The history of Samuel, for example, was not written to speak to and satisfy the sensibilities of modern-era Westerners. It was written to an ancient Eastern audience. It was not playing by the rules of our time; it was playing by the rules of theirs. Whether we prefer our world to theirs does not matter, at least on a hermeneutical level. No, what matters for biblical interpretation is understanding the assumptions and parameters that they were working with.

And that was the inspired conversation—the one that happened between the author of Samuel and his audience. If they are playing by their rules, then we must interpret history according to their rules if we want to understand the inspired conversation.

A TEST DRIVE

Let's give these ideas a little test drive before we move on, just so we can have a solid grasp on asking the right questions of the "history" of the Tanakh.

First, we should note that all the tools we looked at regarding the Torah can and will be in play throughout the Scriptures. Most of them will even transcend the Hebrew Scriptures and be utilized in the Greek New Testament. When we get into the New Testament, we will also acquire some new Greek literary tools and rabbinic practices (more on this later).

So, in the "history" of the Tanakh, keep on looking for chiasmus and parallelism and borrowed cultural context. These kinds of buried treasures may not happen at nearly the same rate in the Nevi'im as they do in the Torah, where they seem to be one of the defining characteristics, but they do show up.

Second, when it comes to the "history" portion of the Nevi'im, I always like to frame my interpretation and exegesis from the posture of "prophetic history." What is the author trying to communicate about God? What is God trying to communicate about himself and his relationship with his people?

We already hinted in the last chapter that Joshua may potentially be a borrowed cultural genre—what many historians call "conquest narrative." It was very common for

Hittite or Egyptian kings to drastically exaggerate their tales of imperial victory (or even reframe a defeat). If you are familiar with the story of Sennacherib, king of Assyria, as it appears in the Tanakh (for example, in Isaiah 36–37), then you would be surprised to read another record we have found where he reframes that humiliating trip back home as having Hezekiah shut up in Jerusalem "like a bird in a cage."[2] These narratives were commonplace for the people of biblical history—similar to a politician's PR stunts or press conferences where people in power reframe and rewrite reality to suit their agendas.

My suggestion is not that any of these books misrepresent reality in the same way, only that they use a genre everyone would have understood to tell the story of God. Some scholars propose that the book of Joshua is far more satirical than we might be comfortable with. They point to the absolute lack of historical and archaeological evidence and corroborating historical details for a conquest on this scale, suggesting that Joshua utilizes the conquest narrative as a literary device to express a much tamer reality of how God's people came to settle in the land.[3] Many of these same scholars suggest that Joshua and Judges are parallel histories of the same period. One is more accurate to the struggles of God's people as they are tempted to assimilate to the world of their pagan neighbors, while the other is a story of victorious conquest and what is possible when you are faithful.

I'm not looking to convince you of either of these opinions. My goal is to help us pay attention to the ways

Hebrew historians would tell history with a purpose—to recognize that more may be happening than a surface reading would suggest.

In these books of the Bible, I prefer to lean toward a more historical reading whenever it's even slightly justified. There's danger in over-allegorizing a story, and I am careful not to identify something as satire unless the device is blatantly employed. However, if these scholars are correct and God wants to subversively reclaim conquest narrative and tell a satirical story of conquest for a purpose, that is completely fine by me. I remain convicted of the absolute inspiration of the Text because inspiration is about the source, not about whether I can make logical sense of what's happening. *Inspiration* means God-breathed—the authority behind the Text, the Author behind the author.

One final example of how our better questions impact our reading of history in the Tanakh: In the record of 1 Samuel, we read about the anointing and selection of Israel's first two kings, Saul and David. Is the author of the story attempting to function as a journalist, giving us unbiased reporting of the selection and behaviors of Saul and David? Well, on a very immediate and practical level, we have to acknowledge that the inspired biblical author is selecting (inspired by God) which stories to include. These records are far from a day-by-day record of each king's life. So, in choosing which stories to focus on, the biblical author has an agenda: to tell us something about the kind of king God desires.

The author could have picked all of Saul's best days and

ignored his worst ones, and we'd have a totally different record. But this author wants us to learn from the history of God's people. These stories are meant to help future leaders not repeat the same mistakes and to guide the readers— God's people—to live differently.

Does the author have a purpose in including the story of Saul as a herder of donkeys, in contrast to David as a herder of sheep? Are there undertones of the kind of leaders they are (what kind of donkey herder loses donkeys?) and how Israel may be acting under each man? In the Jewish perspective, these deeper implications are absolutely present in the story. If the people of Israel were acting like sheep, God would give them a shepherd. When they first demanded a king, God gave them a herder of asses, so they are being . . . ?

Is the famous story of David and Goliath just a news story about the happenings in the battlefield that day? Or are there intentional treasures buried in the story to provoke the reader into spiritual transformation? Consider all the numbers in the story, and how we've already learned to pay attention to the implications of numbers in the Tanakh. Notice also that this story has some problems—namely, disruption in the chronology of the Saul-David relationship (was David already in Saul's service or not?)—which might lead us to look for parallelism. The author seems to be working very hard to tell the story in the way that we see it, indicating that some intentional juxtaposition between Saul and David may be happening.

Why? Because the Hebrew historian is also a prophet.

They have seen their history through the eyes of God—and are trying to tell the story in a way that changes us.

WE KNOW THIS

We should not be surprised or perturbed that Scripture uses history with an agenda. After all, even the most "unbiased" history textbook makes choices about which details to include and focus on. Which pieces of context are relevant, and which are conveniently forgotten? This can be done intentionally or unintentionally, out of constructive or unhelpful motivations, and with positive or negative ramifications.

We know this. And we also know that our modern context is full of stories in art and even in history that shape culture (and hopefully our character). We consciously ask questions about the way we tell cultural narratives and why.

In a movie like *Schindler's List,* real historical tragedy forms the foundation of an unbelievably moving story that shows us who we are capable of being. At the same time, we know that the story was, in real life, full of complexities and nuances the movie cannot portray. The "real" character of Oskar Schindler was no superhero but a normal human being like any of us. He is a great example of integrity, character, courage, and shrewdness, and the story unfolds to highlight those elements.

Most of us would not be surprised that the storytellers chose which events and pieces of the story to tell to accomplish their purpose. We would not be fazed to learn that bits and pieces of the story were slightly rearranged or embellished to make the cinematic experience more effective. We understand this because we understand what happens when history meets art—what happens when human beings bring an agenda to the medium.

The ancient world of the Bible used historical events as a medium to communicate transformative truth. We'll find ourselves asking the questions the Bible is asking if we remember this while we study this portion of the biblical library. If we learn to look for the larger purpose for the story and the lesson that is being taught in the "historical record," we'll realize that the record was never as concerned about what *had been* as much as it was about *who we were becoming*.

Now—at the risk of overcorrecting—I often wrestle with the order of priority in the biblical text. Was their greatest priority accuracy and then the transformation of the reader, or was it the other way around? Is the breath-of-God inspiration of this Text attached to its historicity or to its objective "lesson" in the telling?

Rather than resolve that wrestling match (which I'm not sure is even resolved in my own mind) for you, I will let you wrestle with that on your own as well—for these are the wrestling matches that help us fall deeper in love with the God behind the pages of the Bible.

Bible professor, scholar, and author Pete Enns notes,

The Bible looks the way it does because God lets his children tell the story. . . .

Writing about the past was never simply about understanding the past for its own sake, but about shaping, molding, and creating the past to speak to the present.[4]

As we read the prophetic history of the Tanakh, we are hearing the community of God's people tell the story. And they are telling the story in order to shape and change God's people moving forward—meaning that we should find ourselves changed today. How tragic would it be if we spent all our time defending historical veracity and never let the inspired accounts penetrate our character?

And so, while it's not my intent to suggest that we have to pick between historical veracity and the intended lesson, I do pray that we will take seriously the real possibility that we have often missed the weightier matters of this prophetic history.

May the prophets still speak, even when they wear the title of biblical historian.

RESOURCES REFERENCED

The Prophets by Abraham J. Heschel
episode 206 of *The BEMA Podcast*, which discusses
    the nature of truth in literature:
    https://www.bemadiscipleship.com/206
Elle Grover Fricks talks about the archaeology
    surrounding Joshua in episode 240:
    https://www.bemadiscipleship.com/240.

Episodes 38–41 of *The BEMA Podcast* dive deeper into the David/Saul story as it's seen in the literature of the prophet/chronicler.

A Tale of Three Kings by Gene Edwards

Where God Was Born by Bruce Feiler

The Bible Tells Me So by Peter Enns

FOR FURTHER STUDY

The Prophetic Imagination by Walter Brueggemann

For more on Joshua, see episode 34 of *The BEMA Podcast*: https://www.bemadiscipleship.com/34.

The Old Testament Case for Nonviolence by Matthew Curtis Fleischer

Inspiration and Incarnation by Peter Enns

The Shack by William P. Young is an example of a powerful, provocative story that has the power to change the reader without being historically "true."

CHAPTER 5

READING WISDOM WITH WISDOM

Wisdom Utilizes a Genre with Limits

When did someone finally tell you to tap on the neck of the ketchup bottle, rather than the bulky section where the ketchup is, to get the ketchup to flow freely?

What about the time you realized you'd been struggling for years trying to use a sink plunger as a toilet plunger? Who knew there was a difference?

Have you ever read one of those "life hack" clickbait posts online and discovered that the drawer under your oven isn't for storing cookie sheets and muffin pans? It's designed to keep foods warm until you serve them.

I feel like this gap between practice and purpose is similar to the way Westerners approach wisdom literature. We are familiar with the Psalms—they've been lying around the spiritual house as long as we can remember, and we use them all the time—but nobody ever told us how to get the most mileage out of them. We spend our time trying to grapple with the idea that we are "sinful from the time [our] mother[s] conceived [us]" (Psalm 51:5), or how it's acceptable to sing songs about the death of our enemies.

The Proverbs are great, but sometimes we try to use them for something they weren't designed for. Maybe people around you keep quoting proverbs about how honest friends are better than dishonest enemies or how rich folks have all the connections—but everything seems to feel a little . . . off. Like using a sink plunger on a toilet. It kind of works, but you have this sense that something isn't quite right.

And Ecclesiastes is like that drawer under the oven. It generally works for how you've been using it, but the author may be throwing up a heavenly facepalm because you've missed the actual point.

There may not be a more distinct genre of literature in the Tanakh than the books of wisdom. Their form and function are unique, as is the objective of this part of the biblical library. Wisdom literature is not meant to tell a historical narrative, and neither does it take the form of law or holiness code. Wisdom is a form of instruction with a little bit more depth and mysticism.

My friend Reed Dent observed this about wisdom literature:

> Much of the law and prophets are concerned with
> the collective journey of God's chosen people
> from Egypt to the Promised Land and beyond.
> Wisdom books deal with what happens in your
> family's caravan on the way. They ask: How do we
> live moment to moment, why, and does it mean
> something?[1]

On the surface, wisdom literature can feel straightforward and practical—a collection of clean statements about how the world is. And yet interacting with it feels, at times, a little clunky. Applying the wisdom of Proverbs, for example, is super easy and enjoyable—until it isn't. The songs of the Psalms are exactly what one would expect, and yet the raw emotion can raise some serious theological questions. Ecclesiastes is fine, I suppose, if you're in the right mood.

And just what do you do with Song of Songs? Is this actually erotic literature, or is it an allegorical representation of God's relationship with his people? Is it both? Is there more?

Rachel Held Evans wrote that wisdom is "not just about knowing *what* is true; it's about knowing *when* it's true."[2] Consider how Proverbs 2 clearly states that the wicked perish from the earth, while Ecclesiastes 7 says the opposite. So which is it? Well, it's all about understanding whether that plunger is for the toilet or the sink. (All right, I'll move on from the plunger metaphor.)

READING WITH WISDOM

To make sure we're asking better questions of wisdom litera-ture, we have to start by realizing how incomplete it is as a whole. That feels awkward to write, so I can only imagine what it feels like to read. But wisdom literature is different in how it presents itself.

Most of Scripture gives us the bulk of the "goods" up front, allowing us to analyze the big picture of the passage. Wisdom literature seems to keep most of the content behind a door. It cracks the door open and lets you hear the music inside, but the truth can only be experienced by walking through the door. The depth of wisdom, the mystery of wis-dom, is not something that can be contained in prose—no matter how profound it is.

Dent helps us understand the complexities of wisdom this way:

> While we tend to think of wisdom as a museum
> curator, keeping prized bits of knowledge behind
> protective glass cases so you can learn something
> smart (even if you can't really do anything with
> it), Scripture portrays wisdom as a woman
> calling out for someone to come and engage with
> her. I think of [a] dance partner. Yes, there is a
> knowledge component to it—you have to study
> particular steps and learn [the] technique—but it
> also requires repetition and practice. And anyone

who knows dance knows that in practice there is something dynamic and *lively* about dancing with a partner. Dancing with wisdom—knowing what is true and when it's true has to actually affect your steps. . . .

. . . Wisdom is not knowing what course of action is right but when a course of action is right. What wisdom being lively and dynamic as opposed to dusty and static means is that what's wise is not always wise.[3]

Just look at how the Proverbs present this in two subsequent proverbs. The redactor and compiler of the Proverbs doesn't even attempt to remove the tension by separating the ideas with a chapter or two. No, instead the two proverbs are purposely arranged right next to each other.

Do not answer a fool according to his folly,
    or you yourself will be just like him.
PROVERBS 26:4

Answer a fool according to his folly,
    or he will be wise in his own eyes.
PROVERBS 26:5

Do you see how disorienting this is to our typical "I read the Bible to know the truth" mindset? Which one is it? Am I supposed to answer a fool or not? The Bible literally just told me to do both, warning me that if I don't follow its instruction, things will go badly. And that's just the beginning—once you start to think about these short statements, you have a hundred more questions. Not the least of which is *Who is a fool, and how do I know that I'm dealing with one?*

But it's also here where I begin to understand, deep down, what the proverb is speaking to. Have I ever dealt with a fool? I have. I have engaged fools and watched it go poorly, just as I have ignored them and watched it spiral into chaos. So how do I know what to do? Based on experience, it all comes down to context and circumstances.

Sometimes it's an issue of what is at stake. If you don't do something, who suffers? What is lost? Or is this a situation where doing something will be the cause of suffering or loss instead?

Discerning where the stakes are too high, and acting out of that discernment—this is wisdom.

It's knowing how to dance with the circumstances of life. And this is why wisdom is often (though not always) connected to maturity. The more time I've spent dancing with Lady Wisdom, the more I understand how she works. And I cannot know this by simply watching her from across the dance floor.

I love the image that Scripture employs of wisdom as a woman. When I was pursuing my wife and courting her for marriage, part of the undeniable electricity of the relationship was what she kept "hidden." She was a mystery, emotionally and mentally. Wanting to know what she was thinking and feeling drew me deep into relational pursuit.

I think wisdom is the same way. It has this romantic seduction to it, inviting us into a deeper relationship, demanding that we get to know it if we really want to know it. Wisdom is a woman who is beckoning us to dance with a knowing look. *You can't learn me from a safe distance. If you want to know me, take my hand.*

If wisdom is a dance, wisdom literature can be one of our instructors. And part of discerning how to apply wisdom is knowing what kind of dance steps you need. Each of the books of wisdom—Psalms, Proverbs, Ecclesiastes, and Song of Songs—draws us into a different kind of journey and asks us to dance with it in a different way.

Psalms

Humanity has, for a very long time, been drawn to song, partly because as words set to music, a song can communicate something that those words in isolation could not. Art transcends the rote expression of transferring ideas, and music communicates depth of emotion particularly well. Music is not comprehensive; it does not address all of life's experiences at once. Music requires us to dive deep in a specific direction to find a feeling, explore it, and express it.

When we hear a song expressing hurt or anger, we appreciate what the song is doing and join in the rage. We don't evaluate it from a distance or expect it to speak to the whole of the human experience. When we hear a song about break-ups, we don't demand that it offer the "counter truth" of legitimate love. When we hear a singer rapt in obsessive romance, we don't insist that they remember to be cautious in such pursuits.

Sometimes when we read the Psalms, we forget that they are songs attempting to express human emotions as worship to God. We find ourselves trying to force the words into more comprehensive theological categories. But the vehicle matters because it changes what kind of ride we're on.

Proverbs

The sayings in Proverbs are a wonderful collection of wisdom. But what perspective should we bring to them? I often tell my students that the Proverbs are "wise sayings that are generally true." That is, there are exceptions to almost every proverb, and some proverbs are true only in exceptional circumstances.

So what good is there in a proverb? A proverb is good not because it is universally true but because it prompts us to deeper reflection. The proverb is an invitation to ponder, to examine life by stopping and turning the situation this way and that. It's a life lesson recorded succinctly and directly. Had the author written a treatise on it, that would have ruined the pointed depth of the lesson learned, and you wouldn't be given an opportunity to be changed. There would be no invitation to dance.

Ecclesiastes

Ecclesiastes is another book that has all sorts of layers. And the deeper you go—the more you pull each layer back—the more it seems to twist back in on itself.

On a surface level, the book comes to grips with the futility that rages all around us. On a deeper level, it seems to hint at where true meaning and purpose can be found. On an even deeper level, it starts to talk about how these different ideas interact in application so we can find fulfillment and make a difference in the world.

Somehow, this journey takes us from meaninglessness to the depths of meaning all in a matter of a few pages.

Song of Songs

I often discuss the wisdom literature with my students as a tool bag for the journey. As we find ourselves on this epic quest of life, God has given us some basic tools to help make things a little easier. Sometimes we need little nuggets of life lessons. Other times we need song and emotion. And sometimes we need training in finding purpose.

Another part of the journey involves relationships and intimacy. Bible students often talk about this in general terms; we don't get specific and practical about intimacy in its different forms in our Bible study. And yet Song of Songs is not very general at all. There is some debate about this, but I would definitely say that Song of Songs offers some of the most erotic descriptions of the marriage bed and sexual pleasure expressed between partners. Whether you are examining the anticipation of the wedding or the culmination and consummation of this union, acknowledging the euphemisms that seem to be in play in the pages of this book will make you sweat.

Is this book *just* erotic, though, or does it also offer wisdom? I assume the latter. Wisdom usually operates effectively on a surface level, but it always contains deeper layers of meaning and insight. Could it be possible that Song of Songs is a critique of imperial power—a tale of a king who desires a maiden and a shepherd who truly possesses her heart? Romantic love is a power all its own, and it bows its knee to nothing. There's certainly wisdom in that reflection, among many others.

And this is part of what we've been mentioning all along. These deeper questions, these contemplative invitations, these explorations of what God might be saying and doing through inspired Scripture are what provoke life change as we are "transformed by the renewing of [our] mind[s]" (Romans 12:2). I'm not just talking about cerebral, intellectual "what if" conversations. I'm talking about the opportunity to take something in, all the way into ourselves—and, through intentional study and the Spirit's guidance, *understand what it is calling us to become.* Each stroll through the wisdom literature is packed full of potential to change who we are every day.

Part of asking better questions of the wisdom literature is knowing which piece of literature we are holding. As we seek wisdom in the situation, we need to know what we are interacting with and which book to go to for which need.

This portion of the biblical library is unique because you aren't just reading the story of Samson or engaging a chiastic literary tool. You are being given little keys that require some thought and exploration before you know how—and when—to use them. And each key is unique. Ecclesiastes doesn't always lead you where you want to go, and proverbs are really useful until they aren't. But if you have an intimate knowledge of which keys to turn and when, you'll find yourself opening the right doors as you walk along.

CHOKMAH

Oftentimes when we think about wisdom, we picture the most intelligent among us—university professors in tweed jackets, or old men with long white beards sitting on top of a mountain. And yet, the Hebrew idea of wisdom doesn't have a terribly strong connection to intelligence.

The Hebrew word for wisdom is *chokmah*, and *chokmah* does some interesting things in Scripture. On the one hand, *chokmah* has been around since the foundation of the world. Jewish tradition teaches that wisdom was present with God when he spoke creation into existence. Jewish mysticism gets a ton of mileage out of this idea, and the Gospel of John (as well as other places in the New Testament) might be playing into this concept. But perhaps the most helpful place to start with *chokmah* is Proverbs 8:22-31, where she speaks to us directly (identifying herself throughout the chapter in places like verses 1 and 12):

"The LORD brought me forth as the first of his works,
   before his deeds of old;
I was formed long ages ago,
   at the very beginning, when the world came to be.
When there were no watery depths, I was given birth,
   when there were no springs overflowing with water;
before the mountains were settled in place,
   before the hills, I was given birth,
before he made the world or its fields
   or any of the dust of the earth.
I was there when he set the heavens in place,
   when he marked out the horizon on the face of the
     deep,
when he established the clouds above
   and fixed securely the fountains of the deep,
when he gave the sea its boundary
   so the waters would not overstep his command,
and when he marked out the foundations of the earth.
   Then I was constantly at his side.
I was filled with delight day after day,
   rejoicing always in his presence,
rejoicing in his whole world
   and delighting in mankind."

So *chokmah* is this massive, transcendent idea, right? This passage talks with sweeping, grandiose language about the foundations of the earth and the fountains of the deep. You can hear the thunderous voice of the announcer saying, "Annnnnnnnddddd now . . . *CHOKMAH!*" *Chokmah* seems to be this huge concept that struggles to fit into even the most poetic expressions of theology.

Yes, and . . . well, not exactly. Wisdom shows up in some of the most mundane, ordinary ways as well. When we read the story of Bezalel and Oholiab building the tabernacle, for example, we are told all about their gifted expertise—what Exodus 35:35 calls their "skill." You may be surprised to learn that this skill is actually the word *chokmah*.

So while *chokmah* existed before creation itself, it is also the things we do with attention and expertise—the skills we possess.

At least it can be. But sometimes it's not. Sometimes it's one idea and sometimes it's something totally different. Sometimes it is big and sometimes it is small. Sometimes it's poetry and sometimes it's elbow grease.

This entire discussion of wisdom literature, at least for me, is one of the most frustrating parts of the journey into asking better questions of Scripture. We keep talking about the mysterious abstract and aren't able to pin down exactly what we're talking about. Wisdom is as big as stardust and as small as the blacksmith's sweat beads.

And maybe that's what *chokmah* is all about and what wisdom literature tries to point us toward. Wisdom is the starting point, and it doesn't go anywhere if we don't engage with it on its own terms, in the specific situations we find ourselves in. Or, as Dent put it, wisdom is the seed of the oak tree—yet the table doesn't build itself.

One final reflection from Dent as we close our chapter:

The first main thing to say is that *chokmah* is a woman, uncomely as her name may be. In Hebrew the word is feminine. In Proverbs she is portrayed as Lady Wisdom. *She* calls out. *She* instructs. *She's* a person. And *chokmah*, just like all women, is complex. We want to build *chokmah* like a modern skyscraper: Twenty-ninth floor for moral wisdom. Cubicle 9b for justice; across the aisle is righteousness, yelling at someone on the other end of the line. Going down, fourteenth floor for intellectual wisdom. Philosophy department gets a corner window so they can stare at the infinite blue sky all day long. The wise man has a big brain. No, the wise man has a big heart. Which one is it?

But in the Hebrew Scriptures, such fine delineated blueprints don't exist, just as you can't draw up a working schematic of your mom, girlfriend, or wife. *Chokmah*, she has many facets that blend into each other. There is a distinct quality between knowing what's good and evil and knowing how communities should be ordered and knowing relational principles and knowing how things go together. All those are kinds of wisdom. But they can't separate entirely from one another. If you know how to run a business well, you're wise—you have *chokmah*—but if you use that business for evil gain, you're a fool.

So how do those kinds of *chokmah* intersect? Well, where does my wife's shoulder become her neck? You wouldn't know unless you get to know her, and even then you can't really say. . . . What's the exact midpoint between your sister's tones of patient urging and annoyed nagging? Well, you wouldn't know unless you've lived with her. And even then . . . So, from the outset, as we look at the different facets of *chokmah*, let's just first approach her with the same humility with which we approach mom at the end of a long road trip. And let's see that, even as we observe her, we are being invited past observation to moving in with her.[4]

If all this sounds different from what we said about the Torah or history, that's because it is. This is the point of asking the right questions. We read the Bible better when we realize that each part of the Bible is radically different. We dress differently to engage its different parts. At the risk of being too clever here, we use wisdom in engaging the Text.

Wisdom is a journey into questions themselves. These absolute statements and practical treasures, which seem to be some of the most clearly stated verses in all Scripture, are doorways into depth and mystery.

We ask better questions when we avoid the temptation to simply state wisdom as shallow fact and keep digging deeper into wisdom literature itself. We accept the invitation to come and dwell with wisdom, experience it, and reflect on it. When we go to teach and preach on wisdom, we speak from the awareness of something we use every day—and something that has been around since the foundations of the world.

Rather than rushing into exegesis mode when reading wisdom literature, we ask *chokmah* for a dance.

RESOURCES REFERENCED

"An Introduction to Joy" speaking tour by Rob Bell: https://youtu.be/sA7LmEn3xyc
Word Pictures by Brian Godawa

FOR FURTHER STUDY

The Symbolism of the Biblical World by Othmar Keel
The Voice Bible by Ecclesia Bible Society

CHAPTER 6

PUTTING THE PROPHETS IN THEIR PLACE

The Who, What, Where, When, and Why

"We were best friends for decades, Marty. Now she won't even talk to me!"

The woman was sharing her story with me before I headed out onstage for a speaking event. We had just finished up a long year of quarantine, lockdowns, social distancing, and mask mandates. Not only had COVID-19 killed hundreds of thousands, but it had also wreaked havoc on our spiritual communities, often exposing some glaring deficiencies in our spiritual maturity.

Her story was not unique, unfortunately. Her best friend had been swayed by a myriad of conspiracy theories, many of which were tied to theology. Convinced that the vaccine was the "mark of the beast," this friend had decided to cut off all fellowship with her apostate companion. The explanation had been full of Bible passages from both Old and New Testaments, many of which had been taken grossly out of context and applied to the current state of affairs. Good biblical hermeneutics had gone missing early in the conversation.

"Do the prophets really speak about this?" the woman asked me desperately. "Is this really what we're seeing today?"

The prophets are often where things start to go a little crazy for many Christian readers of the Tanakh. Like wisdom, prophecy is a unique genre of literature. When we read the Torah and what we refer to as history, we probably find it much more difficult (although far from impossible) to distinguish between the two. However, when we get to the wisdom books, and now with the prophets, we begin to notice drastic differences.

If we want to read the prophets better, we must use our hermeneutic of authorial intent to deconstruct a lot of misconceptions. Because of the potential for misusing and misreading the prophets, we should start with a few observations and dangers.

First, *the very packaging of the prophet is different from that of other biblical genres* as we look at it externally. We see a difference in prose and structure, and the delivery system is also different. The "voice" of the prophet is not one of a historical observer, attentive reporter, or biased commentator. No, the voice of the prophet is that of an artist, one well acquainted with poetry and verbal architecture.

The prophet speaks in the voice of an intimate partner or friend, not of someone who has been watching from a distance. The prophet knows the main character intimately and is communicating details that only they could know as a result of their relationship. As we read earlier, Abraham Joshua Heschel referred to the prophet as someone connected to the divine *pathos*.[1] Prophecy truly creates and conveys a message unlike any other portion of Scripture.

Second, *we need to rid ourselves of the idea that prophets are primarily (or even significantly) focused on making proclamations about the future.* That was not the main goal of the Jewish prophet. Rather, it was the pagan world that had such infatuations with the future, and throughout the ages we have merely continued to re-create these ideas in more evolved (and just as fallacious) forms.

While the prophets very rarely set out to make specific declarations about the future, they did, at times, consider the future and the direction of things in order to make very clear points about the present. This isn't to say that the prophets never paint an inspired picture about what is to come—but those prophetic paintings often resemble the literary version of abstract art, with very broad strokes.

A Jewish teaching from the prophets might serve us well here. In Isaiah 2, the prophet is speaking about receiving a vision. The nature of the vision is astounding, but for our point here, I simply want to focus on the words used in the introduction to it. Here are the first couple of verses of the chapter:

> This is what Isaiah son of Amoz saw concerning Judah
> and Jerusalem:
> In *the last days* . . .

ISAIAH 2:1-2, EMPHASIS ADDED

It's the phrase *the last days* that draws conversation out of rabbis. The Hebrew expression means "the behind days," which could be explained in many ways. Maybe those days sit behind the veil of the future, behind what is to come, behind our ability to see. But rabbinic tradition takes the opportunity to explain that God's people have a different orientation to time than pagan nations do. Pagan nations tend to be obsessed with what lies ahead—they are "future focused." Often polytheism leads pagan nations to try to use their idolatry to manipulate the gods and what the future holds.

But—as the rabbis see it—God's people have their backs to the future. They are focused on what they can see with a sense of limited clarity. They set their sights on the portion of time entrusted to them, seeking to learn and reflect. They look backward and at the immediate vicinity of their feet, contemplating the past and the present, all while stealing the occasional glance over their shoulder to see what is imminently approaching.

This posture keeps God's people from being fooled by things they can't possibly discern and allows them to use knowledge from their own experience and that of their ancestors to focus on stewarding the present. This is the same tone and posture that the prophets take in their literature. They speak to the present and reflect on the past—sometimes immediate and sometimes distant—that brought them to this moment in time. They occasionally talk what about is on the horizon—like an incoming judgment from Assyria or the dangerous temptation of making treaties with Egypt. Occasionally they will pull their eyes up to the future sky, talking about the hope of incoming restoration and the love of God, which provides the backdrop of God's chronological canvas. But the focus is on the hearer's ability to heed the warnings and direction for how to live *today*. Horizon gazing is never disconnected from the present experience.

The irony is that we often approach the prophets with the very pagan tendencies they warn us about. This is part of the danger of our Western reference point. We look at the prophets and elevate the passages that speak of the future. We try to parse every nuance and detail and center the gravity of the prophets' words to those ends. Because of this, we often make far too much of what isn't there and read right over unbelievably large portions of the prophetic text. We miss the condemnation directed at God's people for empire building and their lack of attention to justice. Focusing on a future judgement, we overemphasize the condemnations of idolatry because that is what fits our Western narratives of orthodoxy (a term that we use to reference "right belief"). We miss the fact that the prophets are much more concerned about orthopraxy (an idea that speaks to "right practice"). While it's undeniable that both of these ideas have their place in the walk of faithfulness, the prophets' focus is far more tethered to the latter. At times, like in the opening chapter of Isaiah, a prophet will blast God's people for having all their religious belief, devotion, and liturgy perfectly crafted but failing to execute even the bare minimum of God's standards in their behavior.

This second reflection leads us, quite naturally, to our third: *We must be diligent to keep the prophets in their present voice.* A prophet is not shouting into a vacuum, and the message is certainly not penned directly to us. The fiery, blistering poetry of Amos was directed at the northern tribes of Israel. Not only do these words have an appropriate time in history, but they can also only be understood correctly in the context of the northern kingdom, not in the southern kingdom of Judah, the land of the Philistines, or Second Temple Judaism. This is simply good hermeneutics.

But beyond this, once we keep the present voice firmly in mind, we are also drawn away from the mistake of trying to find Jesus in all these Old Testament texts. Generally speaking, the prophets are not trying to speak of a coming figure who will answer all of Israel's problems. While they may paint the occasional picture of a messianic age or—when the context is one in need of deliverance—the figure who would be able to turn the tide of history, they are spending most of their time trying to encourage God's people to be who he has called them to be. They are conveying messages of God's *pathos* to his people, encouraging them to consider their orthopraxy, or lack thereof, and the impact it is having on the world and the people in it.

Christians are often taught to see the prophets as the ones God sent to denounce the nation of Israel as "without hope" until the answer to all their problems would come (which is Jesus, of course). Not only is this objectively not true and exegetically irresponsible (the prophets are insistent that God's people can correct their ways and find full acceptance with God), but it's also full of bad theology— seeing ourselves as those who see clearly and those ancient Israelites as rejected fools (we often call this line of thinking *supersessionism*).

So how can we try to avoid these pitfalls? Well—by asking better questions that will help us exegete the prophets. I don't use these questions in a linear fashion, and I am not suggesting an exegetical process or formula. There are times when some of these questions are more readily relevant than others, depending on the prophet and the reason for the study. But whatever path we take, we'll discover a fairly simple way through the pitfalls of the prophets as we interrogate the Who, the What, the Where, the When, and the Why.

THE WHO

I often find the Who to be the most helpful place to start— and there are, in fact, two *who*s that drive this question: (1) Who is the author? and (2) Who is the audience?

Who is the author?

Many of us feel so detached from the world of ancient Israel that we just see any "prophet" as some gray-haired old man in a robe—a little grumpy, perhaps, and with lightning in his eyes. But each of the prophets were different people. Amos was a fig farmer who was an outsider to his audience (Amos 7:14-15). This matters because he's not a "vocational" prophet; he's speaking to a group who wouldn't even see him as "one of their own," or, I would assume, as close to God as they were. This impacts the way you read his message. Amos isn't a pastor speaking to his congregation. He's a layperson from another denomination. That has an effect on his words.

Jeremiah, on the other hand, is so much a part of his people that their familiarity with him complicates how they hear his message. At one point, they seem to accuse him of being a traitor *because* he's from the inside (Jeremiah 26)— his message is so "anti-inside" that they push him out.

How do we learn about these prophets? Sometimes we know very little, historically speaking. But often it doesn't take much to uncover a lot that helps us better examine what we're reading. A good study Bible goes a long way, as does a trustworthy and updated Bible dictionary. The Internet can be invaluable (check out the resources at the end of this chapter and in the endnotes for some ideas), and even ten minutes on Wikipedia or watching a BibleProject video can do wonders for our education.

Who is the audience?

We ask this question in a very broad sense. As we use our study tools—study Bible, Bible dictionary, the Internet, and more—to understand the audience, many times we'll find that there are debates about the details and the nuances. For starters, a basic understanding of Israel's history of the united and divided kingdom is going to be quite helpful because all the prophets speak through those contexts.

Amos, Hosea, Jonah, and Nahum are prophets who are either directly written to or are indirectly pointed toward the northern kingdom of Israel. They are going to have a different experience with characters like the nation of Assyria than their Judean counterparts in the south. Because the northern kingdom has followed some very questionable leadership from people like Jeroboam, they have somewhat abandoned God's prescriptions in the Torah about the place of worship. Because of their apparent unwillingness to repent, they are the first to be turned over to imperial judgment at the hands of the Assyrians.

Prophets like Micah, Isaiah, Habakkuk, Zephaniah, Jeremiah, and Joel are written more to the southern kingdom of Judah at various times in their history. The people of this kingdom remain centered around proper worship in Jerusalem, but they have long struggled with a corrupt and selfish leadership. However, at times their leaders (like Hezekiah) have drawn God's people into repentance.

Prophets like Ezekiel and Daniel are written to a people

in Babylonian exile, which makes them drastically different from the previously mentioned audiences. Books like
Zechariah, Haggai, Malachi, and—for the sake of our discussion here—Ezra, Nehemiah, and Esther are written to
(or about) a Jewish world ruled by Persia. Some of them are
returning home to rebuild, while others are staying in the
nations to which they were carried.

When we are curious about the author and the audience,
we're able to ask better questions than simply *How screwed up
is Israel, am I right?* or *Where do we find Jesus?* These inspired
correspondences are loaded with teaching and meaning that
we can apply to our context today—but only if we hear what
is happening and interpret it directly into its original context,
unfiltered through our New Testament.

THE WHAT

When it comes to the What, our Western sensibilities can
serve us well and be put to use. Time for some good ol' expo-
sitional exegesis, everyone. Live it up!

Exegeting a prophet, though, is a little tricky. They don't
often speak in propositions. When they do, those words are
drenched in passionate fire and condemnation.

How do you apply such statements to modern audiences?
Either what the prophet is saying feels completely irrelevant
because the conversation is so direct (between prophet
and audience, and we are neither), or the Bible teacher is a
little too eager to pass on that direct prophecy void of any

abstraction (they make themselves the prophet and their audience the recipients).

Here's what we have to do instead: Back up just enough to see all the moving pieces. Notice the prophetic author and his audience. Consider the questions we will discuss in the next sections (again, that's why we shouldn't necessarily progress through the Who, What, Where, When, and Why in strict order every time—there's a lot to keep in mind). Then, utilizing our Western ability to think in the abstract, exegete the original conversation that was taking place between all those pieces. What was the author trying to say? And then, while still holding the original author's message in the historical abstract, imagine how that point applies to the current audience. This conceptual What is the piece that gets to be applied directly; it's the fun part of this whole journey.

I know that all these details can be a little overwhelming, and we can start to feel like we're swimming, so let's try to apply this with an example. Let's use what is probably a very challenging case study to make our point.

If you're familiar with Isaiah 53, the "suffering servant" passage, you've been told that this passage is about Jesus as the Messiah, right? Well, based on what we've been discussing, the answer has to be no. There's no way that what Isaiah was doing with his original audience was talking about Jesus. Now, please don't mishear me: Once we get to Jesus, this passage will burst forward in color to find a perfected meaning—but that interpretation simply won't pass muster for the hermeneutic of authorial intent.

So before we try to ask better questions about *what* Isaiah is saying, let's first wrestle with the questions about *who*. Who is the author? Well, Isaiah is. But the moment we start wrestling with the details of this character, if we're doing honest research at all, we're going to find that there is a massive amount of debate about the authorship of Isaiah.

I know this is making everything complicated, and it would probably be nice if I used a cleaner example— I know—but this is the nature of good Bible study and interpretation, so we go with it.

Now, my job isn't to try to convince you of who authored Isaiah. I have my opinions and academic convictions, and yours might end up being different from mine. Most scholars believe we have more than one author at work in the entire scroll of Isaiah. The number of different authors is debated— some say two, others say three or four, and still others say likely many more. Some of the reasons for the debate have to do with literary analysis, styles of writing, and Hebrew language structure.

For the most part, these theories help explain what appears to be a timeline problem with the content. Isaiah seems to, unashamedly, speak to different eras of Judah's history. Some prophecy (potentially chapters 1–11) seems to come early, even before Assyria is on the scene. Other passages (perhaps chapters 12–39) come during the Babylonian conquest of Judah (give or take, plus or minus some theory). Still other sections (possibly chapters 40–55) seem to be written to a people in exile. And the last part (what remains, chapters 56–66) is directed to a remnant considering and experiencing a return to the land of their predecessors. These sections seem to be drawn together with a little bit of historical redaction that doesn't play like prophecy at all, but more like history (chapters 36–39, for example).

The reason all this background conversation about authorship matters is because of how it plays in the historical setting of these prophecies. Isaiah 53 falls around the culmination of what scholars have called the "servant discourse." In Isaiah 40–55, Isaiah is clearly having a conversation with God's people about their suffering and how God is using it for redemptive purposes.

Numerous times, God refers to Israel, Judah, and Jacob as "his servant" and "the one he has chosen." Chapter after chapter, Isaiah reiterates that God has chosen and called God's people to be used by him. They will be a "light for the Gentiles" (Isaiah 49:6), used to bring healing to the nations. Through their suffering, God's people are shaped into the vehicle God has made them to be, outsiders will be restored, and justice will finally be accomplished.

This entire discourse culminates in Isaiah 53, where the prophet describes this servant—already identified numerous times as the people of God in exile—as the one who will be pierced, struck, and striped. Through that suffering, God's people will be healed.

And yes—we can acknowledge from our vantage point

that Jesus will perfectly accomplish this calling that God gave his people. Through the suffering of Jesus, the prophecy will be *fulfilled*. But none of this takes away from the fact that this prophecy has a direct and more immediate exegetical point.

So, as an astute Bible teacher or student, we want to let these better questions of the Who drive us to better questions about the What. *What is being said, and what does it mean?*

The prophet is telling God's people—who were suffering unjustly for the wrongs of others—that sometimes the way we suffer and how we persevere are what God uses to redeem others. Injustice is a part of our world (though this does not minimize or excuse the pain and harm), but when we suffer, we do not give up and lose heart—because redemption involves all of us doing our parts.

That would be a much more exegetically responsible sermon about Isaiah 53 than the typical projection about what Isaiah was "foretelling." Isaiah was doing very little foretelling at all. Isaiah was exhorting. He was instructing God's people in the way of righteousness. It had immediate application, and that was the author's original and—dare I say—inspired intent.

THE WHERE

The better question of *where* is deeply intertwined with *who* and *when*, so we're going to start with a diagram I created to help us get a sense of the bigger picture.

LOCATING THE PROPHETS: PLACE, TIME, AUDIENCE

Pre-Assyrian	Assyrian	Babylonian	Exilic	Remnant
Amos	Jonah	Jeremiah	Ezekiel	Esther
Hosea	Nahum	Lamentations	Daniel	Ezra
Micah	Zephaniah	Habakkuk	Job	Nehemiah
1 Isaiah	2 Isaiah	Obadiah	3 Isaiah	Haggai
		Joel		Zechariah
				4 Isaiah
				Malachi

There are many details and nuances here that could be debated, but let's touch on some of the components of the diagram.

- **Pre-Assyrian prophets:** This time period is when everything seems to be going swimmingly. The stock prices are up, the economy is good—for the rich and powerful, anyway. Only the prophet connected to the *pathos* of God can feel the impending doom and the grief of injustice. So the stinging words of Amos come, rebuking God's people for their mistreatment of the poor. Isaiah derides the emptiness of their religious piety. Hosea speaks to their covenantal infidelity. No one may see it coming, but, "Woe to you who add house to house and join field to field" (Isaiah 5:8).

- **Assyrian prophets:** I have sometimes seen these listed as "pre-Babylonian" prophets. These books include both realities. In large part, the northern kingdom of Israel fails to repent and is destroyed and deported by Assyria. Books like Jonah and Nahum deal with this reflection. The people of the southern kingdom of Judah, having stayed God's judgment through repentance under Hezekiah's leadership, now find themselves back where they started, as the leadership that immediately follows takes them to even worse places than they were before.

- **Babylonian prophets:** The Babylonian conquest takes a lot of time, so this period will cover many years; prophecies like Jeremiah cover everything from the impending doom of Nebuchadnezzar to the process of surrender and the deportation to the exile. Other prophets speak to different situations during this time period. Those who may still be at home looking over the rubble hear Joel. Those who are reflecting on the philosophical ramifications of justice hear the words of Habakkuk.

- **Exilic prophets:** Eventually, the situation is what it is, and God's people face the reality of exile. Prophetic voices continue to express the *pathos* of God. But now this *pathos* is changing as God's softening heart speaks tender words of encouragement and direct words of explanation through prophets like Ezekiel. Daniel likely does not belong in this column (according to most modern scholarship), but for the sake of a chapter where I have likely challenged so much, I will leave that here for now. The reader will also note that I put the book of Job here as well. Job would easily and accurately belong in the wisdom literature, but some theories consider Job to be an old tale that keeps getting remade; the version we have in our Bibles is likely a reflection on the suffering of exile in Babylon. This makes sense of so many literary details that are simply way too far misplaced for an ancient drama, as is often suggested.

- **The remnant:** While some of these are true "prophets" and others are more "writings," I like to put them here in this column for the sake of asking the *who, what,* and *where* questions. More on this in a bit.

In a lot of ways, this chart and the discussion about time period is very much a conversation about *when,* but for me, it's inseparable from the conversation about *where.* When we ask questions about the *where* of a prophet, we're referring to the geographical location of the audience. Is the prophet writing to the northern kingdom of Israel or the southern kingdom of Judah?

Those "locations" are completely locked into a time of history. After the Assyrian time period, the *where* of Israel has changed dramatically. The exilic prophets are speaking to the people of Judah when they are displaced in Babylon. So asking the question of *where* this prophet is being written is completely connected to the time period and historical setting of the prophet. Amos is written to "pre-Assyrian" Israel in the north and Micah to their counterparts in the south.

But Ezekiel is written to a people sitting in a foreign land. The *where* question makes a big difference in biblical interpretation of the prophets.

THE WHEN

There are many differing opinions on *when* much of the Bible was penned. As I hinted at in the last section, the book of Job could serve as a great example. (My suggestion on that likely ruffled some feathers in one direction or another.) We're not going to dig too much into *when* here, because it's beyond the scope of this book and my expertise to attempt to bring resolution to these academic wrestling matches.

But I bring up the question of *when* because, like all the others, it matters, deeply, for good exegesis. Is this prophecy being written more as a real-time reflection for the period the prophet sits in? Or is the prophet composing a later reflection as they sit in exile, thinking back on who they were becoming and what they should have learned? Many people who maintain a singular, coherent authorship to Isaiah take this latter position.

Is Daniel written sometime close to the Babylonian captivity (as the contents suggest on the surface), or is it penned in the middle of the second century BC, at the rise of the Hasmonean dynasty? These details radically impact the exegetical treatment of such passages.

When it comes to the question of *when*, most literary scholarship will tend to be more liberal and less committed to doctrinal considerations or matters like inspiration. My own position falls more in the middle. For some, I will be too far gone; for others, I will not be exhibiting enough intellectual integrity. Wherever you find yourself on this spectrum, I encourage you to lean into faithful critical thinking. Asking these questions is vital to pursuing better readings of the Bible.

THE WHY

At the end of the day, no matter where we fall on the academic details, this last question about *why* has been one of the most helpful better questions I have ever been taught. One of my favorite books for considering this is *Out of Babylon* by Walter Brueggemann.

Brueggemann suggests that each of these periods of history hosted a different conversation among the prophetic voices. It's what I have come to call "The Prophetic Table." For example, as we read the Babylonian prophets, let's imagine these different writers entering a room and sitting at the table for a dialogue. The question for discussion: What went wrong, leading us to the Babylonian captivity?

Isaiah might get things started by talking all about idolatry and obedience—*it's the simple fact that we didn't follow God and his ways.* Jeremiah would say that Isaiah brings up some good points, but if they don't remember relationship, they may miss the whole thing. God's people transgressed a covenant relationship, not just the rules. *If Judah would restore the covenant relationship with God, they would restore order.* And then

Ezekiel might chime in to say, *You're all missing the point and focusing too much on the past. If we don't cling to God in the present, we'll never be ready to return to his larger plan.*

This conversation represents a larger conversation in the Scriptures, and there is no right or wrong perspective. These prophetic voices all represent unique vantage points, and only when you take them together can you see the entire picture.

In noting this, I'm in no way seeking to diminish the unified message of the Bible. One of the most amazing things about the Text is how unified in thought and direction it is. Yet while my early biblical training strongly emphasized that unity, I was never taught to see the nuances within these different voices—and how those nuances could be used for my current application and context.

Brueggemann took this idea of conversations and pushed it toward what he calls the Persian period. Imagine finding yourself after exile in Babylon, when Persia is allowing you to return to your home—what is your call as God's people? Should you go home and rebuild? Should you stay in Persia?

So Brueggemann posits a different kind of table with a different conversation. Isaiah and Haggai offer messages of return and restoration. Ezra and Nehemiah chime in to talk all about the importance of remaining pure as a people rebuilding the homeland of God. Esther talks about how she believes God called them to live in the Persian Empire for such a time as this. They were, after all, supposed to be a light to the nations. She looks to Jeremiah for help—after all, he told them to settle down and seek the prosperity of the city. But Jeremiah continues to insist on the need to have a vibrant and healthy covenant relationship with God, no matter where they are.

It's a hearty dialogue, to be sure. Which voice is right? Obviously, all of them. But each of them represents a different voice for a different context. The question for Brueggemann is which voice we need to truly lean into for our own application. Not to spoil it, but he suggests that the American context ought to lean into the lessons of Esther, learning from what he calls the agenda of *accommodation-resistance*.[2]

As we continue to grow in our ability to have better conversations with the prophets, mere exegesis no longer suffices. We learn to live in the land of responsible application, which is full of dialogue and far richer to the life of faith. It is these questions of *who, what, where, when,* and *why* that serve as our guide.

MY WATCHTOWER

When I was a young pastor—maybe twenty-three or twenty-four years old—I was pastoring a small congregation, convinced I was helping lay the groundwork for the next age of revival. My Bible college had trained me that "spreading the gospel" meant growing churches and inviting more and more people into the transformative work of Christ. I was swept up into an attraction-based church-growth movement with a dash of "emerging church" seasoning.

To be even more brutally honest (and to let you know

exactly who you'd be dealing with back then), I was sure I was going to be so effective that I'd better start preparing for my *Outreach* magazine and *Christianity Today* photo shoots. I wish I was kidding.

Well, you won't be shocked to learn that none of that happened. In fact, my small church wasn't growing much at all, and nobody seemed to be as impressed with my revolutionary revival as I was. So, like any typical twentysomething pastor, I blamed the people.

One night during this season, I woke up and couldn't fall back asleep. It was close to 2:00 a.m. Remember how many of my early mentors had deep commitments to prayer? One of the ground rules had always been "If God wakes you up in the middle of the night and you are clearly awake, do not ignore this. Go find your Bible, listen, journal, and pray until you hear what God might have for you." To this day, I completely stand by this ground rule—I believe the Spirit of God can and does meet us in the dark and quiet hours of the night.

I flipped my Bible open, and it fell to Habakkuk 2. (Yes, yes, I certainly don't recommend the "random flip" as a good Bible study method. But I believe in the mystery of God and that at times, this is how somebody, without direction, might prayerfully surrender to a listening process. Trust me, I have a much better critique of this situation in mind.) I read the opening verses about Habakkuk climbing up into his watchtower and demanding an answer from God. God responds by telling Habakkuk that he needs to write the vision down. He then says the vision is as good as done. It will come. There will be no delay. It is as sure as the sunrise.

So I, believing that this was a message straight from God, grabbed my journal and wrote down a vision of my own design. I envisioned a megachurch built on the property adjacent to the small, unimpressive building our congregation currently didn't fill. I envisioned a full parking lot and block parties. I envisioned service projects. I'm sure, though I didn't write it down, that I envisioned *Christianity Today* reporters in the lobby.

I then went to church that next Sunday and preached a fiery, passionate message. I rearranged the chairs in the sanctuary to face the windows that looked out onto the adjacent property that we owned. I told the congregants all about the words of Habakkuk and my vision. I had heard from God.

I believe in the mystery of Christ and the movement of the Holy Spirit. I believe that God can use any piece of the biblical narrative to speak to us directly and personally through his Spirit. I believe he can do that through Habakkuk, Leviticus, or 2 Timothy. That is not my criticism.

My criticism is of what I did that day as a preacher, a Bible teacher, and a spiritual leader. I didn't practice good hermeneutics. I wasn't pursuing a good reading of the Bible. I was leveraging experiences to further a selfish agenda that I didn't (couldn't?) see in the moment. I had convinced myself it was from God. I had done my best to convince others of the same. And I dragged the name of God, the Word of God, and the hope of his people into the mess.

There was no church building. No reporters from *Christianity Today.* And two years later, I was moving on to my next chapter of ministry.

Pursuing good exegesis and responsible application of God's Word matters—for ourselves, yes, but also for our participation among God's people.

Today, as I write this chapter, I reflect on a second possible ending to that story. First of all, I want to be gentle with that struggling pastor with dreams and visions—he needed space and time to properly process those things. (I'm grateful for the processing that came through counseling in the years that followed.) But what if he had woken up in the middle of the night, flipped the Bible open to Habakkuk 2, and taken a prayerful posture?

I know—we've just spent a chapter talking about good exegesis and application and looking at history and time periods and audience and author. But all that intellectual digging needs to be done with an awareness of what we're bringing to the table and the dangers of our own subjective desires—especially in the prophets. A prayerful posture means listening for and believing in the voice of God, even if it's in the early hours of the morning. Something very spiritual and maybe even mystical happens as we wait to hear God speak.

And this is where our questions enter. As I imagine myself sitting prayerfully, listening for and believing in the voice of God, I also picture myself wondering why God has led me to this passage. Instead of thinking about *my circumstances*, I consider Habakkuk and the people of Judah. I ask the Who questions. I sense the ancient struggle of God's people, trying to do what God had asked them to do but not seeing any sign that it's bearing fruit. In that dark office study, I realize that I can relate with their struggle.

I consider the Where questions. I reflect on the fact that Habakkuk's audience sits in the ruins of their dreams and hopes for their children; they mourn the abuse and deportation of their friends and loved ones. I gain some perspective about my own circumstances as I listen to God. Maybe I don't have it so bad after all. I'm reminded that I am surrounded by quite the cloud of witnesses.

I consider the When question. I think about how Habakkuk writes out of a place of exasperated anger. I consider the possibility that Habakkuk writes this much later as he reflects on his situation (much like I'm reflecting on my own story with more maturity). I'm not sure which it might be, but all these questions are leading me to a much healthier hermeneutical experience. I'm not going to have unassailable answers, but I *am* immersed in the inspired Text and what it is saying rather than using the Text to say what I would like.

I also ask the Why question. Habakkuk is taking this opportunity to try to convince God's people to trust that there is more going on outside their experience. There are things they cannot see. He is inviting them to more trust, more faithfulness ("the righteous person will live by his faithfulness"; Habakkuk 2:4), and more perseverance.

As I consider this alternate ending, I realize how radically different the sermon that Sunday would have been. I realize how radically different *I* would have been. And I realize that all this matters.

I imagine teaching the people in my church how to read the Bible like this, equipping them to have similar experiences and be a part of a communal conversation rather than being a bunch of individuals studying the Bible in their own personal bubbles. I imagine that church becoming a people of the Text, a people aware of the long line of believers who have preceded them, understanding that they are caught up in something that has been going on since long before them and will continue long after they (and their children) are gone. I picture a people who see the inspired Word of God as something huge and sacred and full of wonder rather than a holy book to be leveraged for the theological agenda that reigns in their day and age.

How we read the Bible impacts us. It impacts all of us.

RESOURCES REFERENCED

The Prophets by Abraham J. Heschel
The Prophetic Imagination by Walter Brueggemann
Out of Babylon by Walter Brueggemann
Brad Gray's teaching on "Back to the Future":
https://walkingthetext.com/ts-episode-007-back-future

FOR FURTHER STUDY

Robert Alter's translation of the Tanakh (particularly the Prophets) and corresponding articles, introductions, and footnotes

The BibleProject is an incredible resource for studying
   Bible books (and more!).
So is "Walking the Text," a similar teaching resource
   created by Brad Gray.
NIV Cultural Backgrounds Study Bible is a great resource.

CHAPTER 7

THE GOOD NEWS ABOUT THE GOSPELS

Understanding the Essentials of the Gospel Accounts

The Judaism of Jesus was not the Judaism of David or the prophets. Things had changed—a lot.

It's a tricky period of history to discuss because I don't like to make too much about "the two Testaments." We don't have two different stories and two different Bibles. It's important to see the biblical narrative as one unified story with a consistent arc. Yet a handful of centuries passed between much of the prophets and the life of Jesus. The impact of this time period on the consciousness of God's people and the setting of Jesus' ministry is immeasurable.

Before we can start talking about tools that help us have better conversations about the Gospel accounts, we need to talk some about the historical context of the world they speak into. A lot changed between the prophetic conversation we were having in the last chapter and the pages of Matthew, Mark, Luke, and John.

A PEOPLE CENTERED AROUND THE TEXT

As the Jewish people sat in captivity, they asked great questions about who they were and what had brought them to that place. While the details and specifics of this cultural evolution can be fuzzy and debated, we do know that a new Judaism emerged from their time in exile. One thing that historians agree on is that religious expression evolves over time, and this is certainly true of Judaism. The "Judaism" of Abraham is obviously not the Judaism of Moses. The Judaism that emerged from Sinai was not the same faith expression that you see in the Davidic kingdom; and the Judaism that returned from Persia is not the same as the Judaism of the past. Just like all faith groups, the Jewish people of God grew, developed, learned, and evolved in the living out of their faith.

On some level, the people of God knew that the reason they were in exile was because they had forsaken the ways of God. They were not living under his covenant and observing the law he had entrusted to them. Part of the reason this was the case was because they did not *know* the laws of God. This is evident in archaeological evidence (as in the case of the dig reports from Beth Shemesh[1]) and in the biblical text itself; at one point, the people essentially find the law in a closet while cleaning out the Temple (2 Kings 22).

The exiled people of God resolved to never let this ignorance happen again and committed to gathering around the Text. Scholars believe that the early assemblies began as organic gatherings of people (we might compare them to house churches) and eventually became called *synagogues* (the word is actually used in Nehemiah). This gathering was in no way supposed to replace or compete with the Temple. Approaching God through the sacrificial system was not the goal of these gatherings. There was no priesthood and no clergy. This was the community of God's people gathered around studying the Scriptures and becoming well acquainted with the words of God.

Eventually these gatherings became more and more institutionalized, and as is the nature of things, these institutions constructed buildings—synagogues. Even the construction and layout of first-century synagogues tell us a lot about the culture they were created to propagate. They include elements of community and social structure—chief seats reserved for the elderly and wise. The buildings were not typically ornate (at least not originally), and any artistic exuberance was usually saved for the Torah closet, where the Jewish communities kept whatever scrolls they might have had. The *bimah*—the small, elevated platform from which the Text was read—was not on a stage but centered in the middle of the assembly. All these things pointed toward the prominence of one thing: *the place of the Text in the community*.

This institution didn't just come with a building—the

building facilitated maybe the most striking characteristic of the whole effort: *the schooling system*. The children would not grow up unfamiliar with the Text. The people of God would teach their own children the Text. They would memorize it together and have it committed to memory as individuals.

There were a few levels to this educational system:

- *Bêt sefer*. The youngest children (ages five through ten) began to memorize and study the Torah. Many kids didn't progress past this level of schooling, and we assume some didn't even complete it.

- *Bêt midrash / bêt talmud*. We don't have enough historical data to make a lot of authoritative statements, but this is the likeliest name for this stage of schooling. Only a small fraction of children moved from *bêt sefer* to this level. The best and brightest students would memorize the rest of the Tanakh and start memorizing many of the traditions that were beginning to form around it (much of which we believe became the Mishnah).

- Finally, the stage of Jewish education where a student applied to study under a rabbi.

From this educational commitment, the rabbinical systems arose (what scholars call "Second Temple Judaism"), serving as the seeds for what would be Talmudic Judaism in the second century (most Jews call this later period of history "Rabbinic Judaism"). For those who follow Jesus, our focus is often on trying to understand the context of the Gospels (Second Temple Judaism) and less on the development of later Judaism under the Talmud.

The term *rabbi* simply meant "teacher." Though the term would not become a formal designation until the destruction of the Temple in AD 70 (hence the rise of "Rabbinic" Judaism), these informal teachers were still deeply revered and honored in Judaism. They had returned from exile with a fire in their bones to know the Text. The most "successful" thing you could do was find a way to keep growing and excelling in the study of the Torah and the rest of the Tanakh.

That brings us to the Gospels. We have to understand the premium the world of Jesus placed on the Text. This will become relevant later in the chapter, but this emphasis on the Text also serves as the basis for people groups like the Pharisees, giving color to and helping us have proper appreciation for their devotion to following the law and keeping their traditions. It's also illuminating to understand that observant Jews had very large portions of the Scripture committed to memory. They were able to engage in scriptural dialogue that far exceeded what we are used to.

THE TIMES, THEY ARE A-CHANGIN'

Even as Judaism continued to evolve, the world around God's people was also changing in drastic ways. Life under Persian rule eventually gave way to Greek rule, then to Roman rule. When Alexander the Great conquered the world, he spread the ideology of the Greek Empire everywhere he went—and Alexander was very good at this.

This Greek worldview is often called Hellenism. Hellenism was the systemization of Greek values into the sociopolitical fabric of the world. It's fascinating when you consider that one man and empire were able to conquer the entirety of the biblical world. How did they have an army big enough to do this? Well, that was their genius.

Alexander believed that the world Greece offered was so good and irresistible that they wouldn't need to rule it with an army. The Greek Empire had redefined the standard of excellence. One of the many implications of this new standard was a reorientation of values that centered on humanity's needs—comfort, security, pleasure. As Protagoras said, "Man is the measure of all things."[2]

To these ends, Greece perfected systems to facilitate humankind's thriving. Some have described these commitments in four pillars:

- **Education:** The Greeks could teach you everything you needed to know, and they could help you become better and better and better. This education is about your continued perfection.

- **Health care:** The Greeks had built a system that could provide you with basic health care as part of the social infrastructure. The "hospitals" were connected to pagan idol worship (most common was that of Asclepius).

- **Theatre:** I prefer to think of this in terms of media rather than entertainment, although there were undeniably aspects of both. This was how the empire was able to influence groupthink.

- **Athletics:** This system of tribal identity (you competed in the games as a member of your guild, your city, etc.) propagated a cultural mentality of competition and one-upmanship.

Even the slightly astute reader will realize that our Western (especially American) culture is unashamedly built on these same pillars. It's beyond the scope of this study to do a deep dive on this, but this is one way the conversation of the Gospels will become more relevant than we realized—if we can learn to ask better questions.

And before we demonize the culture of Hellenism, we should pause just long enough to realize that the existence of these pillars and these elements are not evil. I'm quite thankful for health care and education. I don't think media is an evil in and of itself, and frankly, I enjoy a great sporting event when it's kept in its proper place. What bothered the Jewish world of Jesus was the overarching narrative of human self-centeredness that pervaded the culture around it.

WHAT TO DO

Although everyone could see the problem, not everyone agreed on how bad the problem was, and even fewer people agreed on what to do about it. And the world of the Jewish people was about to get more complex. Rome came onto the scene, perfecting the art and systems of Hellenism and combining those things with imperial military power.

So Judaism was wrestling with their response. *What do you do with or to Rome?* They came up with five basic answers.

Sadducees

Some may know their Jewish history enough to travel back to the story of Chanukah. After Alexander the Great dies, the kingdom of Greece gets split into four parts. The southern kingdom of Ptolemy rules Egypt and the region of Palestine. The far eastern kingdom of Seleucus rules everything to the east. The Ptolemies rule Palestine with some level of imperial indifference. When the Seleucids defeat the Ptolemies and take over Palestine, they impose a much heavier hand. The Seleucid ruler Antiochus heads into the Jewish Temple, provoking a major riot when he sacrifices a pig on the altar, and God's people overthrow their oppressors. (This an oversimplified version of the miraculous story of Chanukah.)

When the Jewish people take over Palestine, they turn to their Scriptures and hand the leadership of the Temple and God's people to the priesthood, known at that time as the Hasmoneans. These people are descendants of Zadok, known as the Zadokim—or, in English, Sadducees. Within the first few decades, the Sadducees become almost completely corrupt and in bed with imperial power.

As Rome comes to power and the Sadducees can see their impending doom on the western horizon, they strike a deal with the son of Antipater, the king of Idumea and the Nabateans. That son's name is Herod the Great, and he becomes the Jewish king of Judea and Palestine through political agreement with the Sadducees.

Herodians

Now, if you weren't part of the ruling or priestly elite, but you essentially supported the Greco-Roman world and what the alliance afforded you, you were part of what history seems to call the Herodians. You essentially believed that you could have your Hellenism and still be devoted to God. I hope most of my readers are honest enough to realize that this is most of us, on some level. We don't believe we have to choose between our health insurance and our Jesus, between our smartphones and our Bible, between our political parties and our church. And yet, even as we talk about it, we can feel the tension.

Essenes

Of course, there were some priests, as there always are, who refused to give in to the corruption. Some of them believed that the system was so corrupt that they could not serve in the Temple, so they swore off their Levitical priestly role. Others did not believe they were free to do that and continued to serve even in defiance of the corruption (people like Zechariah, the father of John the Baptist, a righteous priest; Luke 1). This group formed communities that sought to keep a pure devotion to the Scriptures. While there is a lot of debate about details surrounding the Essenes, we do know from the Dead Sea Scrolls that they were a committed, sometimes fanatical, band of devotees living in all sorts of places. One of those places seems to be Qumran, where we found the Dead Sea Scrolls, which seem to be some of the remnants of their devotion.

Zealots

The rebels who helped overthrow the Greeks and stood for God's way at Chanukah felt disgusted and betrayed as they watched the priesthood sell their soul to the same imperial identity they fought to purify themselves from. This group, known as the Hasidim (the "loving ones") and the "Pious Ones," went up north to Galilee to build towns where they could be completely devoted to living on God's path of righteousness. They planted towns like Nazareth, Cana, Bethsaida, Capernaum, Korazin, Gamla, and Gennesaret. One branch of the Hasidim was radicalized and violent. These people were known as the Kana'im (the word *kana* meaning "zeal"). In English, we call them the Zealots. They looked to Phinehas, Joshua, and Elijah as their role models. They believed that God would save them as they partnered with him in political rebellion, rising up in faithful, violent commitment, just like at Chanukah.[3]

Pharisees

We are perhaps most familiar with another branch of the Hasidim, one that was just as committed to righteous devotion. In fact, the Pharisees believed it was their commitment to religious purity and a righteous walk before God that would cause God to save his people without violent political overthrow. God would do this supernaturally, much like he'd done in the Exodus.

—

Obviously, I share all this because it provides the unbelievably relevant backdrop to the Gospels. Just knowing this backdrop and some of the main character groups helps us ask better questions about what we read. We often talk at length about "the Jews" and Jesus. I hear Christians lump Pharisees and Sadducees together as if they are the same people—while they are on completely different ends of the religious spectrum. Knowing where Jesus is standing and what the cultural status quo is in that area adds depth and richness to the story you are studying. Are the people around Jesus Zealots, ready to start a holy war? Are they Herodians, trying not to upset the Roman politic?

But what about the literary nature of the accounts themselves? How can we ask better questions about that?

A NEW KING AND A NEW KINGDOM

The very word *gospel* has an unbelievably informative context because the "Gospel writers" were not the first people to write about what they called a "gospel." In fact, Alexander the Great was one of the first (and there may have been many more before him).

The term *gospel* can also be translated "good news" and refers to an imperial proclamation that announced a new king and a new kingdom. When Alexander conquered the world, he brought with him a gospel, the "good news" that the kingdom of Greece had arrived. There was a new king and a new kingdom—a kingdom with education and health care and everything your heart could desire.

Later, when Rome came onto the scene, they capitalized on and perfected this art. Whenever there was a new emperor or a change in power, they seized the opportunity to build momentum and proclaim the good news—a "gospel"—that there was a new emperor and a new imperial reality.

When there was a battle for the Roman throne, after the assassination of Julius Caesar, Marc Antony and Octavian had it out. Eventually Octavian, whom history knows as Caesar Augustus, took the throne, and a new "gospel" went out throughout the empire. *There is good news. Rome has a new king and there is a new kingdom, the kingdom of Augustus.*

To make this point, I love to take students to the little storefront temple that a German archaeological team found in the ruins of Priene, in what is now Turkey. In that small temple, a plaque proclaims the following:

Citizens of Priene: Since Divine Providence has brought to life the most perfect good in Augustus,

whom she filled with virtues for the benefit of all
mankind, bestowing on us Augustus Caesar as
Savior of the World, for he has put an end to war
and brought perfect peace. By the epiphany of his
birth, he brought the gospel of peace to all mankind.
For that reason, the Greeks of Asia have on this day
declared that the New Year should begin from now
on, on the 23rd of September, the day of the birth of
this god. Never will another gospel surpass the gospel
that was announced at his birth. He is not only Lord
of the Empire, but Lord of the Earth and of the
calendar and of time itself.[4]

There, inscribed in stone decades before any biblical
Gospel was penned, we have an example of what gospel is
and how gospel functions.

The intentional cultural appropriation by the Gospel
writers means that we'll want to take a similar approach to
the Gospels as we did to the prophets.

First, we'll note that the style of literature is quite unique.
The Gospel writer is engaging in very tongue-in-cheek,
subversive writing—under the ostensible rule of one king
(Caesar) and kingdom (Rome), they are proclaiming that
there is a new King and a new Kingdom. His name is Jesus,
and he has ushered in the Kingdom of God.

You'll find this to be true in a very direct way if you
search throughout the New Testament. John the Baptist is
proclaiming a gospel message: "Repent, for the kingdom of

heaven has come near" (Matthew 3:2). As soon as John the Baptist dies, Jesus takes up the message: "Repent, for the kingdom of heaven has come near" (Matthew 4:17). When Jesus sends the disciples to preach throughout the land, he tells them to proclaim the "kingdom of God" (Luke 10:9). When we encounter the apostles in Acts, they are preaching the Kingdom of God (Acts 8:12; 19:8; etc.), and later we are told that Paul is proclaiming the Good News of the Kingdom (Acts 28:23, 31).

This really is the nature of what the New Testament is try-ing to teach us. Understanding intent is important because, once again, the Gospel writers aren't just recording history: They have an agenda. Each Gospel writer is choosing the stories they want to share and sharing them in a particular way, stringing them together for the purpose of a Gospel. They want you to know that there is a new King (Jesus) and a new Kingdom (a new reality that Jesus has invited us into).

Does our preaching and teaching ask these questions? Are we learning these things in our churches and small groups and Christian colleges and seminaries? Do we hear the invi-tation to live into the Kingdom of God today? Or do we just get told stories about Jesus to prove that Jesus was who he said he was? Are we telling people to "share the gospel," which is actually just explaining "how to be saved" and go to heaven and does not mirror at all what we find in the biblical text? Because that changes the message—and if we're chang-ing the message away from the intent of the Gospel writers, that matters.

All this is a great example of how the Western mind uses the Bible to promote our theologies rather than allowing our theology to be formed by the Text that should shape it. None of this is to say that our theologies are wrong, but remember—getting our weighted priorities out of alignment led to centuries of bad readings of the Bible and a whole generation trying to deconstruct how we got here.

Second, just like we did with the prophets, we want to ask questions like *who, what, where, when,* and *why.* I won't outline each and every one of these questions here, but the same principles apply and are relevant in their own ways.

Let's start by recognizing that the audience of each Gospel greatly impacts the agenda with which the writer was communicating. In the same way that you might pick a prophet because of the voice they bring to their prophetic table, you might find that you want to pick your Gospel based on the writer's agenda and what they were trying to accomplish. It might also mean that "harmonizing" is one of the most damaging things you could do to the Gospels. After all, whether the Gospels can be harmonized is not a question the Bible is asking. A better question is *What is each Gospel author attempting to do with their unique presentation of this good news?*

Gospel of Matthew

It's been very popular to claim that Matthew is attempting to prove the identity of Jesus as the Jewish Messiah, but this framework can be somewhat misleading. While Matthew wants to have a very Jewish conversation about

Jesus' identity as the Messiah, if his goal is to prove how much of a Jewish Messiah Jesus is, Matthew does one of the worst jobs.

To start off, Matthew's genealogy is one of the worst in Jewish record. A Jewish genealogy is written to record the lineage and pedigree of the person in question. You can, on some level, choose the lineage and names you promote to make the person you're writing about look as good as possible. However, Matthew goes out of his way to include women (something that was hardly ever done in Jewish genealogies of antiquity), and not just any women, but those with stories that would blemish the genealogy.

This is the worst genealogy we've ever seen—unless that is precisely Matthew's point. Is his point that Jesus isn't the Messiah that the Jewish world would expect at all? Is the point of his Gospel to call into question all the assumptions we make about what God is up to? When you follow the record of Matthew, you can see that this is the clear theme of his Gospel. Notice the upside-down Beatitudes, the numerous outsiders who are praised and welcomed by Jesus (while the religious and pious are routinely criticized) . . .

When we consider the personal story of Matthew himself, it becomes clear why this is the "gospel" that he longs to bring to the world. There is a new King and a new Kingdom. It's a kingdom where outsiders belong and mistakes don't disqualify you, where everything is backward from what the religious people want you to think, and where a rabbi calls a tax collector like Matthew to participate.

Gospel of Mark

Mark is the shortest of the Gospels, and many people have made some pretty bad assumptions (in my opinion) that it's the first Gospel penned. Church historians (Eusebius, Irenaeus, and Jerome—to name a few) tell us that Matthew was originally written in Hebrew, and I believe that Mark is taking Matthew's bulky Jewish account and making it more palatable for his Roman audience. This is why Mark's account is shorter and punchier. No Roman is going to wade through the Jewish details. This account pops from one story to the next, utilizing the word *immediately* around every corner. Immediately Jesus went here . . . immediately Jesus went there . . .

This Roman Gospel caters to the Hellenistic mind, talking about how all the crowds were "amazed" and "awed" by Jesus. He's an incredible healer (health care), an incredible teacher (education), accomplishing incredible feats (athletics), and a great entertainer and storyteller (theatre).

Of course, this Gospel has an awkward, abrupt ending. If you go to Mark 16, you'll notice that most manuscripts don't have the ending to Mark, and the one that's there now (verses 9-20) was clearly added later by the early church in a probable attempt to clean up what appears to be a mistake or missing parchment. However, if you let the Gospel end where it wanted to (at verse 8), you have a group of women hiding after the Resurrection, terrified and afraid. Why would the Gospel end like this? Because this is exactly where the gospel leaves a Roman audience. Terrified! They have heard a new gospel that is challenging the cultural gospel they're used to. Should they choose to accept this announcement, their true allegiance will be tried—and Rome does not take kindly to imperial competitors.

Gospel of Luke

It's often been said that Luke was trying to give the most accurate (*orderly* is the word he used to Theophilus; Luke 1:3) account of Christ's life to a Gentile audience. There's a chance this might be true. However, while many have pointed to Luke as a Gentile author, Luke would have likely been a Jewish proselyte, since he was present before the great Gentile inclusion. The likelihood of this Jewish identity is bolstered when we notice that the Gospel utilizes unbelievably striking Jewish features and literary tools. Additionally, as far as we can tell, Luke doesn't seem to be the most chronological or accurate Gospel author at all (at least from a Gentile perspective).

One scholar, M. D. Goulder, suggested that Luke was written to be a companion volume read alongside the synagogue lectionary calendar (known as the *parsha* and *haftorah* readings).[5] Again, does this help us ask better questions? It does! Is Luke about Gentile accuracy, or about announcing a new King and a new Kingdom in a very Jewish way, right alongside the weekly readings you're already engaged with? How do those weekly readings "talk back" to Luke's Gospel? There are huge hermeneutical implications to these possibilities.

Gospel of John

According to church tradition and history, John, the "pastor to Asia," set up shop in Ephesus toward the end of his life, providing pastoral leadership to the Jewish-Gentile church in Asia Minor. Some have suggested that John wrote his Gospel to "fill in the gaps" left by the Synoptics. (The "synoptic Gospels" is the name given to the three Gospels that have more parallel accounts: Matthew, Mark, and Luke.) Literary scholars have almost completely rejected this idea. They have suggested that John didn't even have access to (or potentially even know about) the other Gospels. I don't particularly agree with this assessment, and I happen to believe that John's Gospel is very aware of those other accounts. Again, solving that mystery isn't necessary for me in this space. We are here to ask questions; simply being aware of the moving pieces is helpful to engage in critical thinking.

Of course, if John were trying to translate a Gospel for a completely different world, it would make sense that he would pick different stories and tell them in different ways than his apostolic colleagues did. He was attempting to announce a new King and a new Kingdom to the world of Asia Minor. That cultural backdrop was much different than that of the region of Palestine and Judea. The pagan idolatry that drove the cultural conversation was radically different. It would, then, come as no surprise that John would utilize stories with unbelievable parallels in the Greco-Asian world of Asia Minor.

=====

As you dive deeper into the Gospels, know that there's an unfathomable amount of information about literary scholarship and textual criticism to help us ask an endless list of better questions. From premises about textual constructions to how the Gospel may have been designed (eventually) to work together as almost a training of sorts, there are just so many good theories to contemplate in contextual studies.

And if it feels like we only scratched the surface of each of the Gospels, you're right—maybe even only *the surface* of the surface. We're just starting conversations here, just prompting the beginnings of questions that will open up a whole new world of exploring Scripture for you. There is so much more ahead. The rest of those conversations is the work that I hope you will continue long after you're done reading this book.

THE ETHIC OF THE GOSPELS

A generation before Jesus, two rabbis argued ad nauseam about many things, including many things that Jesus directly speaks to. These two "schools" of rabbinic thought were prominent in Jesus' day, and it's clear from the Gospel records that he is purposely engaging them.

The school of Shammai is often identified as the more conservative school of thought, aligning more with an obedience-centered way of reading the Torah. The opposing rabbi, Hillel, took a more love-centric reading of the Torah.

On all but one occasion, when Jesus is asked how he reads the Torah, he sides with Hillel. Sometimes he takes Hillel's position but takes it even further than Hillel does. Sometimes he seems to quote or point to Hillel directly.

Hillel's grandson is Gamaliel the Elder, one of Judaism's greatest rabbis of the first century, the supposed teacher of Paul (before Jesus) and the famous Jewish leader quoted in the book of Acts. Not only does Jesus side with Hillel, but so did Judaism for the ages to come.

Someone more qualified than I could write an entire book on this topic, but being aware of even this much of the Jewish context helps us ask better questions. It informs us of the religious conversation taking place around Jesus and the disciples and gives us a sense of what they are speaking into.[6]

And yet, what stands out most about Jesus' interaction with the larger Jewish conversation in his ministry is that he challenged the way they were reading their Bibles—which, incidentally, is the same thing it should do to us. This means that as we read the Gospels, we should make sure not to interpret Jesus' words through a lens he did not intend. And it means that we should take them seriously through the lens he did intend.

What I mean by that is that I think many of us have become so used to the teachings of Jesus that they no longer have the same "teeth" they originally had. Our familiarity has neutered the points that he made.

When Jesus said that the two greatest commandments were loving God and loving others, he was siding with Hillel, claiming that God desires us to read the Scriptures primarily through a lens of love, not primarily through a lens of obedience. We're used to that teaching, sure. Some of us may even realize that the application of this gets to be a little challenging and provocative. We are quick to assert that these two ideas are held in balance and that love and obedience are not mutually exclusive. Those voices would be right. Shammai and Hillel would also agree.

And yet, Hillel and Shammai would argue that necessity demands that we give one of those principles more "weight." The Jewish conversation identified this as the "weightiness of the law." When push comes to shove, which law rules the day? When you're forced to make a decision on interpreting the law—not just in exegetical theory (orthodoxy), but with your behavior (orthopraxy)—which lens do you use to make your decision? Obedience or love? They are not mutually exclusive, but they are often pushed into conflict. Shammai said obedience and Hillel said love.

Jesus said Hillel was right.

And just when we begin to be challenged by that, we need to realize that Jesus said even Hillel didn't go far enough!

Jesus was pressed on the issue of application one day. He was asked by a daring lawyer to answer the question "Who is my neighbor?" (Luke 10:29). This was a question that Shammai and Hillel argued about as well. For Shammai, the command to *love my neighbor* referred to *my Jewish neighbor*. It did not apply to Romans and other Gentiles. Conversely,

Hillel saw the neighbor as those you live among; this meant that *loving my neighbor* extended to even the Romans.

But let us be very clear: Nobody taught that you were to love the Samaritans.

Many of us know the teaching. Jesus is asked about his neighbor, and he tells a story about somebody in need who is overlooked by the devoted, the pious, and the religious—but seen by a Samaritan. In one dramatic teaching, Jesus challenged everyone's understanding by suggesting a vision of love so radical that their current borders of understanding couldn't contain it.

Even the most loving and inclusive among them wasn't loving enough. Jesus was arguing for a profound change in the human heart. Jesus was arguing for a scandalous belief in grace, mercy, and forgiveness. Jesus was arguing for a love of enemies.

And he did it again and again and again. Until it got him killed.

If you're a follower of Jesus, what Jesus said should matter to you. Immensely. But if we're honest with ourselves, there's still an awful lot of "Shammais" dressed in Jesus' clothes who run around in modern-day evangelicalism. We struggle to live out the love ethic of the Gospels, and I suspect it's partly because we haven't been asking the right questions—of the Text and of ourselves—as we read. How we read the Gospels matters because it should change how we live the Gospels now.

And that is where we turn our attention next because

that is where the Bible turns its attention next. For the rest of the Bible, Jesus' followers will work hard to apply this world-changing perspective to each unique context in which they live.

RESOURCES REFERENCED

The first volume of Ray Vander Laan's That the World May Know series, titled "Promised Land," has some good discussion surrounding the Beth Shemesh dig.

Another great source for this material is the sixth volume of the same series, titled "In the Dust of the Rabbi."

To study the "gospel plaque" I referenced in Priene, search for "Priene calendar inscription."

The Evangelists' Calendar by M. D. Goulder

Interpreting the Gospel of John by Gary M. Burge

The Secret Message of Jesus by Brian D. McLaren

FOR FURTHER STUDY

Episodes 73–83 of *The BEMA Podcast* discuss the cultural setting of the gospel much more in depth.

N. T. Wright is considered by many to be one of the shaping thinkers of "Kingdom theology" and applying our awareness of what the gospel is to the biblical narrative; any of his books that point to the gospel, the Kingdom, or Jesus is a great place to start.

Reading the Gospel of John Through Palestinian Eyes by
Yohanna Katanacho

Kenneth E. Bailey was a great literary expert in the
Gospels.

Any book by Lois Tverberg will be very accessible and
eye-opening.

Jesus engages in other rabbinical techniques that we find
elsewhere in the rabbinical era.[7]

Many Jewish scholars (out of places like Hebrew
University in Jerusalem; scholars like David Flusser
and Shmuel Safrai) have pointed to the clear
principles that exist in the teaching of Jesus.[8]

anything by Brad H. Young or David N. Bivin

Life and Times of Jesus the Messiah, Bible History, and
The Temple by Alfred Edersheim

David Flusser was a prominent authority on Jesus from
a Jewish perspective.

A Rabbi Talks with Jesus by Jacob Neusner

Roots of Rabbinic Judaism by Gabriele Boccaccini

CHAPTER 8

LEARNING ABOUT THE LETTERS

Refusing to Systematize the Theology of the New Testament Letters

You know that person who can tell a great story? One of my favorites is my colleague Jeff Vander Laan (no relation to my teacher). One of many reasons I love Jeff's stories is that he can make a story fit within a larger context. Jeff has worked for our organization for over twenty-five years, so he has many great stories. He can tell stories from his experience as a student, and he can tell stories from his time as a new campus minister or an executive.

Whenever Jeff tells a story, he has a thorough and intimate awareness of our organizational narrative. He knows where we've come from and where we're going. He's seen some significant mistakes and could keep you busy for hours with stories of triumph and celebration.

But no matter where he is in a story, Jeff can see where it fits into the larger history of Impact Campus Ministries. He's always aware of why he's telling the story in the first place.

Have you ever been listening to a story from someone— maybe even somebody who is good at telling a story—but you can't figure out what any of this has to do with what you were talking about? That's not Jeff. Jeff can always connect the dots and make the point.

And the Bible is more like this than many of us may realize.

TELLING THE STORY OF THE BIBLE

One of the big passions that drives the work that I do with *The BEMA Podcast* is increasing our awareness of the metanarrative of Scripture—the big story that God has been telling in the world. For us, our understanding of much of that story is going to emerge from the record as we have it in the Text. The Bible is not necessarily trying to actively present the story as one unified metanarrative—but I do believe that it is helpful, as we interact with the Bible and understand how story works, to be able to see the contents of Scripture within a unified story arc and communicate it to others as such.

So when you read the story of the Torah, you are really encountering the opening chapters of this metanarrative. With my students, I often talk about how Genesis 1–11 functions as the **Preface** to God's story. As in any other series, you encounter a preface that will orient you to the unique parameters of this world. In a series like, let's say, Harry Potter, this is important because Hogwarts is not a normal place.

In the story of God, the irony is that we *are* talking about a normal place—the real world. However, enough bad versions of it have been passed on that we start to see our own world through a very distorted and inaccurate lens. The preface of God's story takes those distorted lenses and reframes the folklore and the story. It cleans up the lens and updates the prescription, inviting us to look at the story through a new set of assumptions.

God isn't angry at us, we're not bad, and this world isn't the result of chaotic collision. Love rules the day, and grace is the foundation of the universe. Trust that story because the antithesis of trust is fear and insecurity. If you let fear and insecurity govern, it very directly leads to sin. And that sin messes all kinds of things up: family relationships, tribes and nations, even entire civilizations. Humans have a long history of not trusting. In fact, it seems like we're incapable of trust.

So ends the **Preface**. Pretty depressing, right? Turn the page to the **Introduction**: Genesis 12–50.

In the **Introduction**, we meet the family of God. They're built from a particular kind of stock; they have a certain kind of spiritual DNA. Following in the instinctual footsteps of a father named Terah, who left Ur and the status quo for something better, a man named Abram demonstrates an unusual ability to trust. It turns out that we humans aren't incapable of trusting, and God was quick to partner with the first family he could find that was willing to give it a shot.

Now, the family is far from perfect, and they make a ton of mistakes. Over the first few generations they struggle with intense dysfunction, experiencing everything from religious trauma to a desire to murder siblings. They deal with the depths of sinfulness and the heights of forgiveness. This entire journey through the **Introduction** leads them into generations of slavery under the boot of empire. Yet the **Introduction** has insisted that there is plenty here for God to build an incredible narrative out of.

This **Narrative** will end up going from Exodus through the Gospels. God will take this family and turn them into a nation. He will take that nation and rescue them from the throes of imperial abuse. He'll invite them into a special relationship, and they'll say yes to the partnership. The mission that they'll embark on together really hearkens back to the opening paragraph of the **Introduction**, when God told Abram that he wanted to use him to bless the whole world; God insisted that all nations would be blessed through this story. Whether they remember that promise or not, centuries later, this nation continues to say yes.

God defines that partnership through the law, leads his people through ups and downs in the desert, and tells the story of it all through Moses before Moses dies. This is the Torah.

God continues to tell his story through the Nevi'im (the Prophets), and we watch this nation struggle on every level. They go from being the bottom of the heap to being decent members at the table of nations to being a group of folks who tragically forget their own story. Instead of remembering what it's like to be slaves, they become the enslaver. God warns them, but they refuse his correction. The fate of the mission hinges on this idea, so to keep it on track, God reminds his partner what it's like to be the slave—again.

As the people reflect on this journey, they also begin to collect their corporate wisdom. They gather all this—their songs, their poetry, their nuggets of wisdom, their erotic literature, their reflections on exile, their perspectives on looking back—and they put it in the Ketuvim (the Writings).

This is what constitutes the narrative arc of God's story. These are the pieces that we've discussed so far, laid out into a coherent and (hopefully) accurate narrative.

Enter into this story the person of Jesus and the announcement of a new King and a new Kingdom. A Jewish rabbi, entering into a Jewish story, reminding God's people of their mission to be a light to the Gentiles, to love their neighbors and their enemies, because this sacrificial love is what it means to walk in Abram's footsteps. The Gospels are the culmination of the **Narrative** of God. Notice that *Jesus doesn't start something new—he properly reframes what the invitation has been.* It's not a new story; it's the culmination of the same one we've been studying.

And the book of Acts becomes the **Epilogue** to this **Narrative**.

The **Epilogue** follows the dramatic conclusion of the plot. It's the "what comes next"—what the characters in the story do following the climax of the narrative. The impact of Jesus ripples throughout the world as the new Kingdom bursts forth.

The Jewish mission of God is being realized through his very Jewish partners, the apostles; they are becoming a light to all nations. Gentiles begin flooding into the story because this is what the story has always been about, all the way back to that opening paragraph in the **Introduction**. The **Epilogue** in Acts is about what you would expect to happen next in the story.

So that is the narrative of God's story told in a nutshell. Genesis through Acts. If I were to put it in a diagram, it might look like this:

THE NARRATIVE OF GOD'S STORY

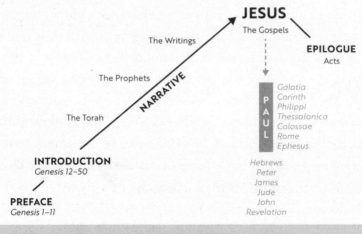

The narrative can be seen in **black** with Jesus as the climax.

The New Testament letters end up being the application of the narrative into particular and unique contexts. For example, when Paul writes to the church in Corinth, he is trying to help them apply the narrative—as seen in Jesus—to their unique situation.

What this means, for all of you who were immediately like, *Wait, what about* the rest *of the New Testament?*, is that the New Testament letters are inspired conversations about applying Jesus and this new Kingdom into the unique contexts to which each is written.

You may remember us talking about *midrash* back in chapter 3. Midrash, we said, was Jewish commentary that provided a way to see and interpret the Torah (and the whole Tanakh) appropriately. One way you could look at the New Testament is to see the letters as inspired, authoritative midrash on applying the gospel.

What does it mean to live out the way of Jesus in Philippi? Is it different than in Rome? What does it look like if I'm in Corinth? Does pastoring a church on the island of Crete look different than it does in Ephesus? Upon reading the letters to Titus and Timothy, apparently it does.

HOW TO THINK

If we've spent any time in church, one of the things that we likely didn't spend enough time on is the idea that the Scriptures are trying to teach us not *what to think* but *how to think*. Understanding this is central to asking better questions of the Bible.

To get a sense of this, let's go back to the Torah and some of the crazy laws we find in Leviticus. Have you ever noticed just *how* crazy they end up being?

Look at Exodus 21:28-34:

"If a bull gores a man or woman to death, the bull is to be stoned to death, and its meat must not be eaten. But the owner of the bull will not be held responsible. If, however, the bull has had the habit of goring and the owner has been warned but has not kept it penned up and it kills a man or woman, the bull is to be stoned and its owner also is to be put to death. However, if payment is demanded, the owner may redeem his life by the payment of whatever is demanded. This law also applies if the bull gores a son or daughter. If the bull gores a male or female slave, the owner must pay thirty shekels of silver to the master of the slave, and the bull is to be stoned to death.

"If anyone uncovers a pit or digs one and fails to cover it and an ox or a donkey falls into it, the one who opened the pit must pay the owner for the loss and take the dead animal in exchange."

Were bull gorings a regular enough occurrence that they warranted this kind of attention? Other parts of the Levitical code go into depth about elevated platforms with parapets. While I would expect this attention to detail for an OSHA safety training, it seems odd to find in Leviticus, does it not?

But the Jewish understanding is not that God is trying to provide every law that you will ever need. Instead, the law is trying to teach you how to rule and how to live. It gives you some outlandish laws and absurd situations, as well as some straightforward and mundane principles, because these provide you with all the parameters you need to know.

The Text is teaching you *how* to think, not *what* to think. What that means is that *the Text is leaving much of the thinking up to us.*

This is super helpful on multiple levels and in many ways because it helps us ask better questions. Not just *What am I supposed to do?* but *What is the principle I'm learning here? How do I take this from here into other places? And what other places?*

This same mindset lies behind (and is taken into) the midrash. God is always inviting us into a physical participation, a "reigning with" him in his Kingdom. This is endlessly relevant to a world that is trying to apply the gospel, an announcement of a new King and a new Kingdom. There is a co-reigning, a partnership in which God is asking us to engage and join him in the restorative work. He isn't just issuing orders—he's inviting us into the process alongside him. This isn't a New Testament idea at all; it's actually a very Jewish way of thinking and living. And it makes sense when we realize that the early New Testament community is led by Jewish apostles and finds itself within a larger Jewish cultural context.

SO, WHAT ABOUT THOSE LETTERS?

So—we have been taught how to think through the Torah. We've seen it done well and poorly through the history and the prophets. We've seen the people of God reflect on where they've gotten this wrong in the wisdom literature and tell stories that help preserve some of these perspectives in the Writings.

And now we also see all this perfectly lived out in the person of Christ, who—without flaw or blemish—lived out a perfect interpretation of this story. If there was any question about what to think or how to interpret that passage or this idea, we know now. We have seen Jesus.

The fullness of God was pleased to dwell in him, Paul said (see Colossians 2:9). He was the exact imprint of God, the author of Hebrews reflected (see Hebrews 1:3). To use one of my favorite quotes from pastor and author Brian Zahnd:

God is like Jesus. God has always been like Jesus. There has never been a time when God was not like Jesus. We have not always known this, but now we do.[1]

The Gospels, the records of the life and ministry of Christ, served as the perfect "buck stops here" interpretive tool. But still, even now, we are not excused from the task of participating. We are still being asked to think. And now, in Christ, we know for sure *how* to think.

When we come to the letters, what we see is the apostles engaging in some apostolic application of Christ into each context. They did not intend for their letters to go together. They were not trying to form a systematic theology. Nor would it be accurate to say that these letters would contradict each other in application. In other words, they aren't written to work together, but they aren't going to work against each other either.

We have to keep these letters in the same hermeneutical lane of *authorial intent* that we have used for this entire journey. Again, the journey through these letters should not be driven by our Western theologies, which were refined in the Middle Ages and built on Greek philosophy. Our journey should instead be guided by the voice of a first-century Jewish teacher, speaking with Jewish assumptions into the world of his audiences.

When Paul writes to the Philippians, he is attempting to help them apply the gospel to their unique context in that moment of history. When James writes his letter, he has an entirely different audience in a completely different context. Their goals are the same: *Apply the gospel.* But their unique contexts, voices, and applications change greatly.

This is why Paul can practice one thing in Rome when it comes to releasing women for ministry but then encourage Ephesus, a context drenched in pagan-goddess worship, to do something entirely different—even the opposite of what was done in Rome. This is because the goal is the same. The New Testament letter writers are not trying to create an abstract system of theology that functions in a vacuum. They are not forming a moral code. They are applying the same gospel—an announcement of a new King (Jesus) and his new Kingdom—to unique places.

This helps us understand what Paul intends when he says, as he does to the Corinthians, "This is the rule I lay down in all the churches" (1 Corinthians 7:17). Paul is saying that there are universal principles that help us know how to think and apply the gospel in our context. However, applying those universal principles would look different in Galatia than it would in Corinth.

Also, understanding the context gives us perspective on those other passages where Paul adds personal clarification. Aren't those passages fun for people like me, who talk about all Scripture being inspired, and then Paul, in inspired Scripture, says, "This is me speaking, not the Lord" (1 Corinthians 7:12, author's paraphrase)? What do you do with that? It wouldn't be so bad except for the fact that Paul definitely wants you to see whatever he's saying as not "inspired, set in stone" words. So what do you do?

Here's how to sit with it: Paul is having a conversation about applying the gospel, but he realizes that there are a few ways of seeing this particular issue—and ultimately, those believers in that context will have to decide how to think about it. Paul gives his perspective but leaves room for their own. Is this conversation inspired? Of course. The whole process is. But the process is concrete, not abstract. It includes the decisions that need to be made in that unique situation, recognizing the need for different decisions in different situations.

So when Paul writes Corinthians, he's not trying to make it relate to his letter to the Galatians—just like when I wrote separate emails to a podcast listener and my coworker about plans for our ministry, I wasn't trying to make those emails work in tandem. I was on the same mission for both emails, but my application of the conversation was different.

When we read the letters, we're eavesdropping on conversations where the apostles taught their audiences *how* to think, not just *what* to think. James, John, and Peter were all apostles. All of them wrote letters, and each of those letters was helping their audience apply the gospel to their unique context. This is why their letters work together perfectly, but never as a unified system of thought. Never as a fixed, New Testament "code of ethics."

These observations can lead to much better questions—and those questions can help us learn to contextualize.

THE COMPLEXITY OF TIME

As we have shown and hinted at throughout the chapters so far, each set of tools we are given grows and expands as history continues to unfold. If you can remember that overwhelmed sense you had when we unpacked the first literary tools in chapter 2, notice that all those tools have traveled with us—and we just keep adding to our toolbox as we walk through history. Our toolbox is starting to get quite heavy, but we're almost done, and we might be able to clean some stuff out before the journey is over. Hang in there!

You know how we started by talking about chiasms and borrowed history and parallelism? Well, all those things are still in play—some more than others—as we read the Gospels and the New Testament letters. Kenneth Bailey filled up a book with chiasms in Luke alone.[2] I think I've found chiasmus at play in over half of Paul's letters (and there are probably more I haven't discovered). The Greek language has a similar but different literary tool called *inclusio*. (Have fun looking that up—you'll love the better questions that emerge.)

Every time we turn a page of history, we bring our tools with us and pick up a few others. We still have narratives written with prophetic agendas (hello, Gospels and Acts). We still have deeply mystical traditions that find themselves rooted in wisdom. Paul and James seem to love a good dance with *chokmah* every now and then. Asking *who, what, where, when,* and *why* is never going out of style. And it's really easy for me to see a prophetic table where first Matthew, Mark, Luke, and John sit, and then John, Peter, James, and Paul.

These new tools enable us to have better conversations. We are journeying and growing and becoming more aware. This will take lots of time, but we're picking up some of the initial data we need to begin.

NEW WRINKLE FOR THE DAY

Okay, Marty, you might be thinking. *So the New Testament letters apply what we've already read. It's more of the same.* Well, no. What would be the fun in that? This is where we get to lean into the problems and ask ourselves an interesting question: *What kind of new wrinkles do we find in the letters, and what questions can we ask of them?*

One wrinkle that I'd encourage you to explore is a new

field of New Testament study that has been growing since we found the Dead Sea Scrolls. The school of thought was originally called the "New Perspective on Paul" and was trying to square some of the things we were discovering in the Dead Sea Scrolls with what we read in Paul.

Paul's relationship with the law of Moses always seemed a little inconsistent, particularly given what we read in the book of Acts. The Dead Sea Scrolls contain evidence that certain language employed by Paul was used in the first century to refer to the law through a particular lens—so what we *thought* Paul had been saying *was inaccurate*.

One of the Dead Sea Scrolls, titled the *miqsat ma'aseh haTorah*, or "The Works of the Law," helps us understand some things about how first-century Judaism understood the Torah. Much of this was relevant to an argument about the Gentiles that Shammai and Hillel were engaging in.

The Jews had broken down the law into three sections:

- **Cultic law:** The part of the law that has to do with liturgical worship at the Temple. This is the Levitical system of priesthood, sacrifice, and Temple worship.

- **Ethical law:** These laws are universally true for all people. Ethical laws are the way God made the universe to function.

- **The *miqsat ma'aseh haTorah* ("The Works of the Law"):** This is the part of the law that makes you Jewish. This includes circumcision of males, keeping kosher, wearing tassels, not wearing blended fabrics, and so on.

Shammai had decided that you were justified—you were declared righteous (please note, this has nothing to do with salvation)—when God saw you being obedient to the *miqsat ma'aseh haTorah*. This would mean that a Gentile would have to become Jewish and begin observing all three parts of the law.

But Hillel said God declared you righteous when you believed—just as God had done with Abraham in Genesis 15. This would mean that carrying out the *miqsat ma'aseh haTorah* was a function of being Jewish, not an expectation from God in order to be justified.

Do you see how that might give us a richer, more colorful, and more nuanced understanding of how Paul talked about justification?

Decades of studying this and positing ideas has led to a more refined, more consistent understanding of Pauline theology, though New Perspective scholars still land in a lot of different places. In more recent years, this continued exploration has given rise to what's been called the "Paul within Judaism" camp, which has (in my opinion) brought an even more consistent reading of Paul. This awareness, combined with many of the resources recommended at the end of this chapter, will be very helpful as we ask better questions of the wrinkles we discover throughout the letters.

And all this doesn't touch the observations that are made outside that realm of study. Here are some other helpful areas to pursue in your quest for better questions:

- How does Paul see "the Christ," and how does he employ the term *Christos*? How does this use differ from other New Testament authors, particularly in the Gospel accounts?

- How many of Paul's letters were written prior to the Gospels, and how did the presence of Pauline teaching shape the formation, design, and use of the Gospels?

- Look into the scholarly debate surrounding Paul's usage of *pistis Christou* ("faith in Christ" versus "faithfulness of Christ") and consider the implications on New Testament theology.

GREAT STORYTELLERS

The thing that makes my friend Jeff a great storyteller is his ability to understand the power of a story and how it relates to the conversation at hand.

Far too many of us have forgotten that the Bible is a great story crafted by a great Storyteller. We've treated it like an abstract morality code that finds its ultimate fulfillment in the teachings of Paul. To quote Brian McLaren, much of Christianity has decided to accept Jesus as our Savior but

Paul as our Lord.[3] We find the teachings of Jesus to be a little esoteric, a little confusing, and not nearly as handy as Paul's imperative Greek language.

We can see clearly what Paul is telling us (or at least we think we can—yikes!) and we settle for what appears to be clear teaching rather than the teaching of the rabbi who bears the name of Jesus. I've even heard people teach a hermeneutic that says you interpret the teachings of Jesus through the teachings of Paul, because you should always interpret the "less clear" passages through the "most clear."

But that whole reasoning is unbelievably flawed because the clarity is simply based on our perception from where we sit. We end up choosing which passages have more clarity— again, to avoid any confusion—rather than understanding which teacher has more authority: namely, Jesus. To use language from the last chapter, we need to remember that Jesus is our ethic and Paul is our missiologist; evangelicalism usually swaps those, making Paul our ethic and Jesus our missiologist.

I'm sure Paul would roll over in his grave if he knew others used his teachings to interpret those of Christ.

Instead, Paul was doing the same thing for all his audiences: using the teaching and life of Christ to interpret for many people in many contexts how to walk in faithfulness.

As we interact with the teachings of the New Testament, let's commit to being better storytellers. Let's work to understand the larger narrative arc of the Bible. Let's work as hard as we can to see Scripture *as it emerges through the person and life of Jesus*. And then let's study the words of the inspired New Testament apostles as they apply that story to their contexts.

Jeff will often tell his stories about Impact Campus Ministries in ways that center around prayer because that is one of the distinctive characteristics of who we are. At some point in nearly all his organizational stories, Jeff says, "And the only thing that was different was the fact that we had prayed."

It's an anchor point in the stories he tells. We walk away having been reminded of a foundational part of our identity.

The refrain of the New Testament could be framed similarly: *And that's the difference that Jesus makes in your context.*

When we hear the conversations of Philippi and the conversations of Corinth, when we realize that Peter and John are conversing with their audiences about the difference that the gospel makes for them, when we hear the announcement of a new King and a new Kingdom sent to the region of Galatia and we do the work to discover the unique things that these audiences were dealing with—I believe that we will start to see these stories within the larger metanarrative. And, as we do, they will help us begin to understand how to apply this same gospel to our own unique contexts.

Because God isn't trying to teach us what to think. He's trying to teach us how to think. And he's inviting us to co-reign with him as he brings shalom to our world today.

There's still work to be done after the exegesis. And that may be the most important part.

RESOURCES REFERENCED

Again, watching how an Orthodox Jew interacts with the Torah can be experienced at places like alephbeta.org. Followers of Christ will quickly realize that the exegesis is applied in different ways than we are used to.

the Covenant and Conversation series by Jonathan Sacks

Understanding the Jewish Roots of Christianity edited by Gerald McDermott

Paul through Mediterranean Eyes by Kenneth E. Bailey

FOR FURTHER STUDY

A great book that dives into this dynamic relationship (of how to think rather than what to think) is *With* by Skye Jethani.

In Search of Paul by John Dominic Crossan

Again, N. T. Wright is a great starting place to read about Paul in context.

So are Ben Witherington III and E. P. Sanders.

Paul among Jews and Gentiles by Krister Stendahl

Other names in the "Paul within Judaism" camp include (but aren't limited to) Mark Nanos, James Dunn, Paula Fredriksen, and Amy-Jill Levine.

I would also recommend Jen Rosner or Mark Kinzer's
    works when you start to wonder about the
    relationship of Messianic Judaism to all this.
The Book of Acts in Its First Century Setting series by
    Eerdmans

CHAPTER 9

APOCALYPTIC REVELATIONS

Reading Apocalyptic Literature
without Losing Our Minds

It's hard to think of a time in recent history when there hasn't been some mass Christian hysteria and fear concerning the end times. Whether it's Hal Lindsey and the sociopolitical scenario of the 1980s, Y2K at the turn of the millennium, the political turmoil in the early 2000s, or COVID-19 and the conspiracies about vaccines, one thing is certain: You can connect any social setting and talking point to the book of Revelation if you want to.

Apocalyptic literature is one of the most unique and often abused genres of biblical literature, not least because we too often limit it only to the book of Revelation. In many ways, we should have covered this genre earlier in our journey together because realizing that apocalyptic literature has a place *long before* Revelation will be essential to asking better questions of the book written by John.

Apocalyptic literature exists within a particular niche of the experience of God's people in history and is often directed at people groups in exile or those experiencing intense persecution. As we discussed in chapter 4, part of the reason the biblical authors utilize different genres of writing is because art can communicate ideas in a way that transcends logic. When somebody—an individual or people group—is experiencing unimaginable tragedy, sheer logic and reasoning don't translate. For centuries, humans have wrestled to explain suffering philosophically, theologically, and sociologically, and in the right spaces, some of those conversations have value. But one space where they don't is where people are going through the tragedy itself. Many of us have experienced this firsthand.

In the midst of deep pain or despair, we cling to ideas and experiences that seem to transcend the logic on the surface. We gravitate toward that which can express the intangible— those things that are deeper, wider, and more substantial. Because of the transcendent reality of these things—like hope, justice, vindication, and the triumph of goodness— explanations and rote theology won't accomplish the task. We turn to expressions like music, poetry, painting, and drama. Art sustains and inspires us when mere definitions cannot. We inherently understand this; we describe art with words like *powerful* and *convicting*. Art provokes us and moves us, meeting our needs for the moment—and sometimes meeting needs we didn't even know we had.

One of the artistic ways prophetic voices tried to communicate to the people of God was through *apocalyptic literature*. The term *apocalyptic* literally refers to the idea of "unveiling."[1] We've talked before about the fact that many people in the Western world have assumed throughout the ages that the prophets were unveiling the future. We can become obsessed with the ability to understand what is coming and believe that every prophetic voice is oriented toward that end.

But the prophets are unveiling a lot of other things, most of which are rooted in experience and oriented very much in the present tense. We may see an unveiling of God's intentions or purposes. We may see an unveiling of things as they truly are—things that seem good may be exposed as dangerous or evil. Things that seem problematic may be exposed as good. And things that are simply hard to see in tragedy are clearly made known.

Unveiling is illumination. Light shines on something that was hidden. The veil is pulled back, the light shows us the nature of what is in front of us, and now we see more clearly.

Many of us have experienced this unveiling in our own tragedies. Now, remember—we're not talking about logic here. Very rarely has any of us been given an explanation that made everything make sense. But if we go back and consider that moment of clarity, of revelation, we realize how this works.

You ran across that movie, and the world was never the

same. Why? Because something had been unveiled. You had been given a gift, and now you "see the world differently." You heard that song, and it opened up your eyes to some spiritual reserve you didn't know was there. You were inspired.

This is what apocalyptic literature is designed to do. While this genre may offer some broad explanations of what the audience may be experiencing, these "explanations" are not rooted in expansive logic and reasoning—they are rooted in art and imagery. Apocalyptic literature takes big, simplistic truths and ideas and wraps them up in artistic, complex stories and images so that they no longer sound simple.

In a similar way to almost every other Eastern tool we've examined, apocalyptic literature is like a treasure hunt where the author has buried something—in this case, something simple but very powerful—under layers of complexity so that when you go through the process of discovery you're able to see something you would have never noticed had you been told it straight.

HOPE UNCOVERED

If apocalyptic literature isn't (mostly) forecasting some distant future—if it isn't an end-times riddle for us to solve—what is it? Let's try to establish a working description to use going forward: *Apocalyptic literature utilizes symbols and images to convey hope to the audience's present day.*

We have to start by deconstructing our previously held assumptions about how this genre relates to the end times.

These rampant misunderstandings are what cause us to anchor this genre to the wrong place and get our interpretations all wrong. In large part, the authors of apocalypse are not trying to prophesy about future events and how the world will end—at all. So before we even touch on the book of Revelation, let's examine some of the biblical apocalypse that existed in the Bible centuries before John's writing. We find this genre of literature in the Hebrew prophets and in writings like Ezekiel, Daniel, Zechariah, and even employed within other prophets, like Isaiah. What we learn from those writings will give us a road map for what to do with Revelation.

Ezekiel

We briefly mentioned earlier that Ezekiel, whose name means "God strengthens," is here for a message of encouragement. Whether we see his name as a reference to the strength that he'll need for his vocational call (which will hardly be a bed of roses) or a nod to his inspired attempts to strengthen God's people— or perhaps both—his named identity is more than appropriate.

Ezekiel sets out to unveil some truth (notice that I didn't say "the answers") about some questions: *Why are we here (in Babylon)? What did we do to deserve this? Has God forsaken and abandoned us?*

These are some of the thought processes that can take tragedy and make it a lot worse, spinning a person into depression and shattering mental health. As an act of survival, the ancient prophets corporately engaged in this experience with reflections on the place and function of faithfulness. A straightforward reality check would be uncompassionate and horribly ineffective. So Ezekiel sets out, inspired by God, to do something unique.

Ezekiel isn't concerned with forecasting future events and how they will go down. He is most certainly not laying out a blueprint for the sociopolitical directions of future (modern-day) empires. Ezekiel is trying to talk to the Jewish people about their *current* world and the *current* situation. And he uses symbols and images to artistically and provocatively communicate his message of hope to the people of God.

Ezekiel 4 is an excellent example of this. Ezekiel is no author, by the way—he's a thespian. He takes his apocalyptic imagery and uses it to perform what I once heard a teacher call "guerrilla theatre."[2] Ezekiel is going to run into a busy part of town, enact a prophetic message from the Lord, then jet out of there at a dead sprint, leaving the "audience" to discuss the prophetic word with their mouths gaping. In Ezekiel 4, Ezekiel is told by God to build a model of Jerusalem, showing the siege that will be laid against it. Ezekiel will be invited to lie on one side and then another, symbolizing the time that will be spent in exile. He will be commanded to cook his food over human excrement but then—after bargaining with the Lord—will be allowed to cook it over animal feces instead.

Like I said, fun calling. He's going to need some of that namesake.

But Ezekiel is trying to communicate hope to God's people. Now, we might immediately begin questioning how this horrible job could possibly communicate hope. Well,

Ezekiel's ministry spans a great time of Israelite history. Ezekiel starts his ministry as Jerusalem is being overthrown; he is there for the exile, and then there to offer words from God after the dust settles. And through it all, one of the things that Ezekiel offers is at least some semblance of *explanation*.

Again, this prophetic explanation isn't the work of logic and reasoning—it's an unveiling of poetic insight. Ezekiel presents simple truth, packaged in a way that can be received and reflected on. Just as I might take time to explain to my young children *why* they are in time-out, Ezekiel takes time to explain to God's kids why, in part, they are experiencing this turmoil. I believe that is one way punishment differs from discipline: Punishment is just about retribution, but discipline is about learning. Discipline makes us stronger; Ezekiel offers strength.

Ezekiel also offers *assurance*—all throughout his prophecy, starting in chapter 1—that God has not abandoned his people. He has, according to Ezekiel, gone with them into Babylon (Ezekiel 10). God has not left them; the presence of God that departed from the Temple now dwells with them in exile. Ezekiel also promises the people that the same Presence will return and dwell in the Temple again (Ezekiel 43). That isn't a prediction of future events nearly as much as it is a message of hope in their current situation. The focus is not on the mechanics of how it will happen or the details of when but simply the assurance that it *will*.

Ezekiel gives strength through *encouragement* and tells people to continue to press forward and carry on.

- There are lessons to learn from our mistakes.

- There are promises to hold on to. We must believe that things are bigger and better than our current circumstances.

- There are reasons to press on into tomorrow. We must believe that we can be a part of putting the world back together.

Ezekiel uses the mind of an innovator, the creativity of an artist, and the imagination of a storyteller to communicate hope to the people of God. They, too, must be creative. They, too, must be industrious and discerning. They must be determined and stubborn for God's ways. The very thing that made them a stiff-necked people in the desert is what's going to get them through this tough time.

But they must endure. They must overcome. They must be strong.

Daniel

The other prophetic voice of hope that found its way into the period of exile is the voice of Daniel. (We've briefly touched on the fact that most scholarship suggests that this apocalyptic book should be placed in a completely different period of history, but for now—and since it doesn't hurt our understanding of the function of apocalyptic literature—we'll keep Daniel placed in our conversation as an exilic prophet with Ezekiel; this will help us understand the shift we'll address in a little bit.)

Many of us will be somewhat familiar with the stories in the book of Daniel. The accounts of Hananiah, Mishael, and Azariah in the fiery furnace (you would know them as Shadrach, Meshach, and Abednego, but please, stop calling them by the Babylonian names given to humiliate them and use the Hebrew names that give them an identity within God's people); Daniel in the lion's den; the Daniel fast; and the vision of the statue are all prominent stories from this book.

But Daniel has so much more taking place under the surface. Daniel is one of the only books to be written in two languages: Daniel 2–7 is written in Aramaic, while the rest of the book is written in Hebrew. Aramaic was the "language of the land" (or maybe more importantly, the language of an oppressed people); it's what everyone in that Semitic portion of the world spoke and could be looked at as the secular language. Hebrew, however, was the language of God's people—the language of the homeland.

After giving us a brief introduction in Hebrew, the writer switches to Aramaic for the first half of the book. This gesture is an amazing literary tool in and of itself. The simple language change gives the reader the subtle impression that *we have lost our identity*. But the book comes down the hillside of hope in the language of Hebrew. You almost sense the message of restoration and hope without any of the content—just the language choice alone. Artistic choices like these are what drive apocalyptic literature.

But wait, the first half of the book is in Aramaic and the last half is in Hebrew? The first half and the last half?

Could we have another chiasm on our hands?

Indeed, we do. Not just any chiasm, mind you, but an incredible double chiasm. First of all, the Aramaic portion of the book of Daniel is chiastic. You might be able to see the chiasm like this:

DANIEL CHIASM A

A1 image of the Kingdom / four-part statue (*Daniel 2*)

    B1 will not worship / thrown into furnace (*Daniel 3*)

        C1 fall of Nebuchadnezzar (*Daniel 4*)

            CENTER justice and goodness / abuse of power and hope of justice (*Daniel 4:37*)

        C2 fall of Belshazzar (*Daniel 5*)

    B2 will not worship / thrown into den of lions (*Daniel 6*)

A2 image of the Kingdom / four beasts (*Daniel 7*)

The center of Chiasm A is Daniel 4:37:

"Now I, Nebuchadnezzar, praise and exalt and glorify the King of heaven, because everything he does is right and all his ways are just. And those who walk in pride he is able to humble."

Excellent. The first chiasm speaks to the justice and goodness of God, something that all the prisoners in exile are questioning. It also speaks about the abuse of power and the hope of justice. This chiasm has it all. But there is also a second chiasm, formed by the Hebrew portion, that symbolizes the return of God's people.

DANIEL CHIASM B

A1 prophecies about beasts (*Daniel 8*)
    B1 trials and forgiveness (*Daniel 9*)
        CENTER sixty-two "sevens" / Anointed One / war and desolations (*Daniel 9:25-27*)
    B2 trials and mourning (*Daniel 10*)
A2 prophecies about kings (*Daniel 11*)

The center of Chiasm B is Daniel 9:25-27:

"Know and understand this: From the time the word goes out to restore and rebuild Jerusalem until the Anointed One, the ruler, comes, there will be seven 'sevens,' and sixty-two 'sevens.' It will be rebuilt with streets and a trench, but in times of trouble. After the sixty-two 'sevens,' the Anointed One will be put to death and will have nothing. The people of the ruler who will come will destroy the city and the sanctuary. The end will come like a flood: War will continue until the end, and desolations have been decreed. He will confirm a covenant with many for one 'seven.' In the middle of the 'seven' he will put an end to sacrifice and offering. And at the temple he will set up an

abomination that causes desolation, until the end
that is decreed is poured out on him."

Now, there's a passage that has gotten some mileage in the
end-times conversations. And for Jesus followers, we certainly
can see Jesus in some of the imagery. I don't want to take away
from that for a moment. But we have to remember that Daniel
wasn't written to twenty-first-century American Christians. It
was written to ancient Jews struggling in the grip of an empire.
What did the original writer mean when he wrote it?

Frankly, the passage just doesn't make much sense if
Daniel is an exilic prophet. How is the message of restoration
of the Temple, the corruption of a King, and the destruction
of the Temple (again!) supposed to bring hope to the people
in exile?

There may be a few ways to answer this question, but this
is where we get back to the discussion of current scholarship
around Daniel. The book makes much more sense if it's written
in the context of Greco-Roman oppression and the corruption
of the Sadducean priesthood that we talked about in an earlier chapter. Try going back and assuming this book is written
about the world that exists just after the story of Chanukah.
Indeed, the message of hope begins to be "unveiled."

If modern scholarship is right, then Daniel artistically uses
the backdrop of Babylon to speak to the current events of the
day. The author frames the current, Greco-Roman exile to the
exile of Babylon (the exile of more recent memory). In doing
this, the writer does something very similar to what we will see

in Revelation. The writer says, *We have been here before, and we are still here. Where is Babylon? Fallen. Where will Greece and Rome be? Fallen as well. But the Kingdom of God? Everlasting!*

But, back to the chiasm. If we have this staggering double chiasm, then it stands to reason that this double chiasm would form a third and greater chiasm, which I will call Chiasm C. Is your head spinning yet? It should be—the writing of the book of Daniel is phenomenal in its depth and artistry. Let me lay out the BIG POINT chiasm of the book of Daniel for you. The center of this chiasm is held throughout Jewish thought, almost without exception.

DANIEL CHIASM C

A1 prologue (*Daniel 1*)

  B1 prophecies about kingdoms (*Daniel 2*)

    C1 God's people in suffering (*Daniel 3*)

      D1 fall of a king (*Daniel 4–5*)

        E1 God's people in suffering (*Daniel 6*)

          F1 prophecies about beasts (*Daniel 7*)

            CENTER vision of a leader establishing an everlasting Kingdom (*Daniel 7:13-14*)

          F2 prophecies about beasts (*Daniel 8*)

        E2 God's people in suffering (*Daniel 9*)

      D2 fall of a king (*Daniel 9*)

    C2 God's people in suffering (*Daniel 10*)

  B2 prophecies about kingdoms (*Daniel 11*)

A2 epilogue (*Daniel 12*)

The center of the book of Daniel (Daniel 7:13-14) was one of the most rabbinically discussed passages of the Second Temple period. The moment you see it, you will immediately recognize it from the prominence it has in Jesus' teachings. Here it is:

> "In my vision at night I looked, and there before me was one like a son of man, coming with the clouds of heaven. He approached the Ancient of Days and was led into his presence. He was given authority, glory and sovereign power; all nations and peoples of every language worshiped him. His dominion is an everlasting dominion that will not pass away, and his kingdom is one that will never be destroyed."

Daniel gives a prophecy of hope that at some point, a leader will come and establish a new Kingdom, one that will never pass away. In the meantime, God's people are left to stand strong in the face of suffering. To resist the pull and tug of empire. To stand and subvert a kingdom that attempts to make you bow to gods that are not your own. Daniel promises God's protection and rescue. Daniel promises God's presence. And Daniel promises a future and a hope.

Notice that this promise is very vague, general, and broad. It makes a statement about a general truth the Israelites put their hope in. It does not provide the blueprint for how the future will unfold. And it's much harder to abuse this section in the same way that we do the "seventy 'sevens'" of Daniel 9:25-27.

But no matter when Daniel was penned, and no matter where you feel most comfortable in this conversation, we have discovered a better conversation to have regarding apocalyptic literature.

So . . . what is Daniel's apocalyptic message of hope, conveyed through the artistic use of language and fantastical stories of dreams and visions? *As strong as these kingdoms and empires appear to be today, they will fall. One by one, each of these kingdoms will give way to the next. Pride is ultimately the thing that will bring them down—and every king will exalt and glorify the Kingdom that lasts forever.* And so, with faces set resolutely toward tomorrow, God's people set out to plod forward until the day they might see "one like a son of man" coming in the clouds of heaven.

Zechariah

Zechariah is another prophet who employs very heavy and intentional use of apocalyptic literature. At the risk of redundancy, I'll repeat that Zechariah's intent is not to lay out blueprints for the future or explain the end times. Whatever God decides to do in the future remains to be seen. God does seem to love cross-referencing his own book, but the original inspired intent of these prophecies is to encourage hope among Zechariah's own audience.

Zechariah is a prophecy about the remnant who have returned to their homeland and the need for them to persevere in the face of imperial rule. Trying to rebuild the glory of "the good ol' days" while under the control of a Persian government begins to weigh on a person's psyche. Zechariah tells them to hold on, and he does so through metaphors, visions, and images.

As is true with much apocalyptic literature, the pictures are often full of symbols that represent God and his people, the trials of the audience, and the eventual triumph of God's good agenda. Also typical of apocalyptic literature, the prophecy begins with images that encourage faithfulness and endurance, then closes with the assuring proclamation that a new Kingdom, a new reality, a new Ruler is on the way. Zechariah is quite insistent that if God's people persevere, their future King will come to them. But for now, they must walk obediently the path that lies before them—the path through Persia.

Notice again how the focus and emphasis is on the people's current life, not the coming King. The promise and picture of a future Kingdom is broad and poetic and speaks of the qualitative aspect of this King and Kingdom, not the mechanics of the future itself. It doesn't outline the *how* and the details—it outlines the *kind of King* and Kingdom we will see.

Having a grasp on apocalyptic literature and the movement of the prophet allows us to understand books like Zechariah as we read. We love to cherry-pick passages that fit our needs for a good proof text, but we rarely find these passages used in context. For example, you may recognize one of the most famous passages from Zechariah:

Rejoice greatly, Daughter Zion!
　　Shout, Daughter Jerusalem!
See, your king comes to you,

righteous and victorious,
lowly and riding on a donkey,
    on a colt, the foal of a donkey.
I will take away the chariots from
    Ephraim
and the warhorses from Jerusalem,
and the battle bow will be broken.
He will proclaim peace to the nations.
    His rule will extend from sea to sea
    and from the River to the ends of
    the earth.

ZECHARIAH 9:9-10

The sun has not set on many Palm Sundays without that verse being quoted at least once—and for good reason. But we often fail to understand Zechariah's original intent when he prophesied those words. Zechariah was insisting that if God's people would find a way to live obediently *within empire*, God would send them rescue. And this rescue wouldn't come through armies and military might but by God's divine providence.

They would see their King rise to power through humility.

Sound familiar? And no, I'm not talking about Jesus. We will certainly see this later in the story, but at this point in the narrative, Jesus isn't here yet. We have to hear this story *in its original context* in order to appreciate what Jesus would do with it. If we do that with this passage, we will likely hear a similar exhortation to what we covered in chapter 6 when we discussed the "suffering servant": people rising to redemption through humility, perseverance, and the willingness to suffer for a greater good.

If the people of God will walk in obedience—even in the midst of Persian rule—God will do something in the world that will destroy the weapons of war and the chariots of oppression.

One final note before we start heading toward the book of Revelation: Almost all the images of Zechariah will show up later, in the book of Revelation. John will borrow the apocalyptic images of the Tanakh to craft his own message to the early church.

SIMILAR IMAGERY IN ZECHARIAH AND REVELATION

Zechariah	Revelation
Zechariah's prophecy starts with a man walking among the myrtle trees (chapter 1).	Revelation starts with a man walking among the lampstands (chapter 1).
Zechariah speaks of the horns sounded to scatter Israel (chapter 1).	Revelation speaks of trumpets sounded to usher in destruction and rescue (chapter 8).
Zechariah speaks of a measuring line used to measure Jerusalem (chapter 2).	The same image is employed in Revelation at the end of the vision (chapter 11).
Zechariah talks about clean garments of the high priests (chapter 3).	John tells us about a multitude in clean, white robes (chapter 7).
Zechariah tells us about a scroll (chapter 5).	John tells us about a scroll (chapter 5).
Zechariah speaks of a woman in a basket (chapter 5).	Revelation speaks of a woman on a beast (chapter 17).
Zechariah contains a vision of four groups of horses (chapter 6).	Revelation contains a vision of four horses (chapter 6).

We stand around and wring our hands and moan about how the book of Revelation is so vague and complex and hard to understand. Yet everything in Revelation had already been said centuries before. If we want to better understand the Text, let's learn how each genre works and how the different books in that genre talk back and forth to each other.

A BOOK FOR ITS TIME

What this largely means is that we read Revelation with the same basic hermeneutical principles we've been using throughout this entire book. We're going to stay disciplined and resist the urge to start losing our minds over this one book at the end of the Bible. We seek to learn *authorial intent*, which means we want to know (as much as we can) what the writer meant when he wrote it and what the audience understood when they read it. This is the inspired conversation.

To these ends, we're going to do our best to understand how this genre of literature functions. We'll realize that apocalyptic literature is not new but was utilized in the Tanakh more than a few times. We can also remind ourselves that the same genre was also employed outside the biblical text in many apocryphal settings. The point? People were used to this genre. It was not alarming or confusing to the original audience. If somebody handed you Shakespeare today, you'd know how to read it. In the same way, the first audience of Revelation knew what they were reading and what to do with it.

The original readers would have started looking for colors,

numbers, beasts—all sorts of apocalyptic indicators that served as a literary key, like the legend on a map, and would help them unveil the message that was being conveyed.

This isn't to say that the Spirit doesn't move as we read the Text today. This isn't to say that there aren't many applications of a Text throughout history, including today. This isn't to say that Revelation doesn't have anything to offer about the future or that God won't do things in the future that line up with the things described in Revelation.

But *Revelation is not written primarily about the future.* Revelation is not primarily about the end of the world. Revelation is written to a first-century church being persecuted by the Roman Empire—to a people who are running for their lives, standing up to the narrative of empire, watching the execution of their brothers and sisters, and wondering if it's all worth it.

To them, John uses apocalyptic literature to communicate a clear message: *It is worth it. You have to overcome because we know how this story ends.*

For some of you, getting to the book of Revelation has been something you couldn't wait for. The anticipation of studying Revelation can be distracting. Others of you have avoided the conversation of Revelation like the plague. You find the whole conversation far too tense, loaded with problems, confusing, and discouraging. My mother is convinced that this isn't a conversation she has to figure out, and she's just going to let it be.

On some level, I can appreciate that. This world (and the

church) could use a lot more of the humility that comes from being okay with not knowing.

But alas, I think we often let ourselves off the hook far too easily, plugging our ears and not wanting to engage in a conversation that makes us uncomfortable. The truth of the matter is that what we believe about "where this is all headed" or "what's going to happen at the end of the world" has more of an effect on what we do day to day than many of the other things we believe. *What we believe about the narrative of Scripture shapes how we live within it—and nothing shapes a narrative more than the ending.* This is why asking better questions of Revelation is so important.

Here are some principles to guide you as you continue to grow in your interaction with Revelation:

- **Remember that there is nothing new in Revelation.** This might be an overstatement, but it is truly just a technicality. There is hardly a single employed image that is not taken directly from elsewhere in Scripture, whether it is from apocalyptic letters like the ones mentioned previously in this chapter or images drawn from the Exodus or the Jewish people's time of exile in Babylon and Persia. Remembering this keeps a few things in front of us. First, we're pointed in the right direction. John was constantly reminding the original audience that they had been here before. Revelation was not a look into the future but in the opposite direction—it was a reminder from their past. Second, we can employ the rabbinic principles of allusion and callback to see what treasures John is leaving buried in his apocalyptic message of hope.

• **Increase your familiarity with the Tanakh.** If we're going to move comfortably around Revelation (and much of the New Testament), we need to be committed to learning about the Hebrew Scriptures, which serve as the basis for its assumptions. Luckily, the Internet will make up for mountains of shortcomings here once we learn how to ask new questions and utilize the tools that are available to us. I don't share this to heap on the guilt or condemnation but simply to make a point: To an evangelical world that usually prides itself on how well we know our Bibles, we have an awfully long way to go before we can engage the Text like the original audience did. More on this in our final chapter.

• **Really search the historical, cultural context of the book of Revelation.** One of the most unique aspects of John's Revelation was his cultural awareness and how, just like in his Gospel (discussed in chapter 7), he tailors the message for his audience. I'll list some great sources for doing this at the end of this chapter, which will open the door to ask more and more questions in the same areas. Not only will you learn that there is nothing new in Revelation from the perspective of the Scriptures, but you'll also discover that every image is perfectly clear in the cultural setting of the audience.

As you move through Revelation 5–6, you see the images of a throne room and hear the sounds of coronation. As the One who sits on the throne and the slain lamb and his authority are described, you realize that this subversive literature isn't describing heavenly visions of the future— John is exhorting the early believers to remember who is in charge and who is truly King. As one friend of mine likes to summarize this section of the book: *John says that he's been to the throne room of God; he's seen God's throne, and Caesar isn't on it!*

If you investigate the context of the first nine chapters, you'll notice all sorts of parallels to the Roman athletic games—too many to be a coincidence. This means that the book of Revelation is cast as a great competition, a great Olympic Games between the Dragon and the Slain Lamb. You may not discover these things right away with a quick Google search. But just as we've said in almost every other chapter, we are learning how to have a different conversation. As we go deeper into the conversation over time and these things begin to become second nature, we'll discover increasing layers of meaning and wonder.

As the story continues to set up different competitions and "events"—all calling back to and drawing, without fail, on ancient apocalyptic literature from Jewish history—the story has many bleak twists and turns. John isn't here to ignore the reality of persecution and people dying for their faith. He isn't glossing over the reality of war, plague, and famine. He knows that these experiences can make anyone question who is really "winning" in these heavenly games. John's apocalypse speaks to the darkness because that is where his first audience needed to find hope.

Eventually, that hope is realized. The entire encounter is over as quickly as it started. The dragon (and all evil) is simply thrown into a lake of fire. There's no colossal fight scene, no wondering whether good will triumph (like in the climax of a Marvel movie). There is just the victory of shalom and goodness over sin and evil.

The book closes with a couple of chapters that truly are about the future. Drawing on the poetic imagery of the prophets, John describes a world where everything is as it ought to be. We don't get specific details or mechanics of how or when it will happen. Like all the other pictures we are given, this one is general and broad, an image of intangible hope. It's a reaffirmation of the story that God's people have trusted for centuries.

This hope is the shining closure to the book that we call the Bible. What Revelation ultimately leaves us with is not a glimpse at the future but an encouragement to persevere and walk faithfully in our present.

And this, for many, can be a better reading of Revelation.

RESOURCES REFERENCED

The Christian History Project published a twelve-
volume series called The Christians; the first two
titles (*The Veil Is Torn* and *A Pinch of Incense*) are
particularly behind my work in this chapter.

The Seven Cities of the Apocalypse and Roman Culture
and *The Seven Cities of the Apocalypse and Greco-
Asian Culture* by Roland H. Worth Jr.

Christ and the Caesars by Ethelbert Stauffer

When I mention online tools available to us today,
I am referring to things like blueletterbible.org,
biblegateway.com, and biblehub.com, to name a few.

We discuss Revelation in depth in episodes 174–189 of
The BEMA Podcast.

FOR FURTHER STUDY

The Days of Vengeance by David Chilton
Reading Revelation Responsibly by Michael J. Gorman
Escaping the Beast by Michael Burns
Jesus for President by Shane Claiborne and Chris Haw

CHAPTER 10

THROWING DOGMA TO THE DOGS

*Understanding How Our Theological Filters
Influence Our Interpretation*

Now that we've spent time adding all kinds of tools to our Better Questions Toolbox™, we need to step back and take a brief coffee break. We need to take some time to be honest and assess where we are and where we're headed.

First of all, we feel a little overwhelmed. Our toolbox is now super heavy. It's hard to carry around, and it's not even as full as it will be as we continue this journey beyond this book. We can't imagine taking it everywhere we go in the Bible. The whole thing seems a little unrealistic.

Second, we're super unfamiliar with the tools that we've added. We read the chapter and we've ordered some additional resources. We did some quick Google searches and read some

Wikipedia articles to make sure Marty wasn't crazy. We've been excited at how our minds have been blown and how the Scriptures open up when we ask different questions. We've even been encouraged to find that there's a whole world out there that has been doing this for ages. But we really feel ill-equipped to use these new tools, and we have no idea what we're doing.

Third, we almost feel like we've gone backward a few steps. We used to know what we were doing, and now we've discovered that maybe we didn't know nearly as much as we thought we did. On one hand, we feel like this is the beginning of a beautiful new chapter, but on the other hand, it feels like we've gone all the way back to square one. Now we have all sorts of new doubts we never had before.

And, by the way, we're starting to feel guilty about all the ways we may have misled others—our churches, our children, our family, and our friends. Some of us have been pastors or had seasons in church ministry. Some of us have led Bible studies. Some of us homeschooled our children and were quite insistent on at least a short list of "questions the Bible isn't asking." Is God mad at us? We're kind of mad at ourselves.

═══

Okay, that was good honesty. We should probably top off our coffee and take a little seat to talk this through. Let's start at the bottom of that list and work backward, shall we?

The fact of the matter is that we've gotten some stuff

wrong. This is a natural part of life and our development as humans. We learn things. And learning things means that we were either ignorant of or wrong about some stuff.

In the Western world, and even more so in the Western church, we're pretty good at going through this learning process in a way that shields us from all the uncomfortableness. We don't like to be humiliated. So we often adapt the learning process to conceal the fact that we should not be as supremely confident as we are. We find ways to center ourselves as the experts.

That's why humility (not humiliation) needs to show up with intention in these places. Being utterly convinced of our rightness hasn't worked out well. Pride doesn't look good on us. We're designed to look good in the humility of Jesus. When we join him in the posture he modeled, things are "right" in the Kingdom.

Therefore if you have any encouragement from being
united with Christ, if any comfort from his love, if
any common sharing in the Spirit, if any tenderness
and compassion, then make my joy complete by being
like-minded, having the same love, being one in spirit
and of one mind. Do nothing out of selfish ambition
or vain conceit. Rather, in humility value others above
yourselves, not looking to your own interests but each
of you to the interests of the others.

PHILIPPIANS 2:1-4

One of the ways we can continue growing is by embracing the natural humility that comes with the learning process. Ten years from now, we will all know more than we do today. What that means is that there are things we are ignorant of and wrong about right now.

Think of someone younger than you, someone you care about very much—your child, a niece or nephew, someone you mentor. Whatever age they might be now, when they were young, you adjusted expectations to their level of maturity, right? You didn't expect a two-year-old to conduct themselves like a twelve-year-old. You don't expect your preteen nephew to have the emotional maturity of his forty-year-old mother.

I can't imagine that God loves us any less than you love that person (so much more, even!), and I can't imagine that he sees us any less accurately than you see them (more accurately—perfectly, in fact!). I don't think God expects any more out of our spiritual maturity than we do from those still growing up around us. He adores us and just wants us to steward who we are well.

Of course you are growing. That is a good thing, a human thing. And your maturity isn't static. This journey has shown you some places where you need to continue to mature in the way that you hold your faith and walk out righteousness. You didn't know, and God didn't expect you to. But you know now, and God is excited about the good work he's doing in you.

But what about that part where we're frustrated with ourselves? Well, I want to encourage us to see ourselves in the light of our growing maturity and also see ourselves *from* our growing maturity. The part of us that is frustrated with ourselves is connected to our shame and insecurity. We don't like to be less than perfect, so when we are confronted with that reality, we want to turn that frustration somewhere—and we often turn it against ourselves. But this isn't healthy, and it's not reasonable. We can't throw a tantrum just because we encounter parts of ourselves we don't like. If we accept the human frailty of others and God does as well, we ought to do the same for ourselves.

And if we can accept our growing maturity in emotionally healthy ways, then it keeps overflowing into more development. Yes, it might often feel like we've gone a few steps backward. It might even feel like we're regressing. This is part of the grieving that comes with healthy awareness. But grief is a sign of growth. As we mature, we become increasingly able to see a bigger and bigger picture.

Sometimes my family and I head out on road trips. When my children were very little, we'd never mention the multiday car ride ahead of them. We had to keep their eyes focused on the next stop. But as they grow, my children become more and more aware of all that is involved in these journeys. As their awareness grows, it can feel to them like they have taken major steps backward; now they know that they will be in the car for hours. Wasn't ignorance bliss? Maybe, but it was still ignorance. What they've gained is a healthier awareness of all that lies ahead and what is going on around them.

The same happens spiritually. It's not that you've gone

backward; it's that you're growing. You see more, and you see more clearly. And all this growth leads to a healthier and healthier posture. Because you see all this, you take a less arrogant, less ignorant, and less immature posture in your discussions and your leadership.

What about those regrets about how you thought and led in the past? That same awareness—that growth—will keep you from repeating your past mistakes. Because you've seen so many new things, you're going to hold your hands a lot more open and be far more considerate of all the things that could be out there. You've heard the fullness of the song, not just the pounding of the bass chords in the left hand. The sheet music is a little overwhelming, but you're walking through life with a newfound sense of awe and wonder. This posture makes you a more open person, a humbler steward of what God is doing in you and around you.

Through this whole process, you're becoming a healthier, more loving person, in regard to both yourself and others. And this was always the greater goal, not the acquiring of Bible knowledge or even better hermeneutics. Those things were a means to a greater end. And that end is the work Paul was confident Jesus was bringing to completion. This changed-you, transformed-you, more-like-Jesus-you is the real treasure. Bible knowledge is overrated. Intimacy with Jesus is what needs to grow.

Our new toolbox can be intimidating, no doubt about it. But I suspect encountering these tools has changed you—and will continue to change you. And now that you're aware of the vast landscape to explore, I think you'll begin to notice the toolboxes others are carrying. As you do, you'll be far more compassionate and understanding. You'll notice that some people are carrying the same old toolbox. You'll recognize the broken tools that are inside, the ones you used to carry. You'll also see that others are carrying toolboxes that look more advanced; they're utilizing tools you've never heard of. This will not surprise you; in fact, you've learned to expect that.

Of course, as you look around, you might notice people with the same model toolbox as you and the same tools, maybe with a few different brands here and there. You notice that they seem much more familiar with their tools than you are with yours. They move them around with ease, and things have become second nature for them.

But, of course, this is to be expected as well. If you look closely, you'll notice that their toolboxes are a little weathered, with some dings here and there. These people's tools bear the marks of character, of familiarity, of regular testing.

You may not yet know how to use all these tools. But you will.

Chances are that a few of those other folks with the same toolbox will help you. You may find yourself able to set up shop next to them so you can just watch what they do. You'll continue learning. And I bet that the next time the opportunity comes to upgrade your tools, the experience will feel more informed and more natural.

Of course, this toolbox is heavy! Which means it's time to make an important point: *You don't need to carry every single tool.* It may be time to rummage through and see if there's anything that you need to let go of to lighten the load and enable you to take better care of the tools you have.

RUMMAGE SALE

Each of us—whether we are aware of it or not, whether directly or indirectly—is part of a faith tradition. It may be the church that we belong to or the institution that trained us and shaped us or the homeschool curriculum our family used. But every one of us has been shaped by some kind of faith tradition. Many of us may even be patchwork quilts of theology, woven in and out of different traditions over the decades. And much of it is beautiful.

But those traditions all had lenses that filtered the way they saw things and which categories they used for the Christian experience. In the Western world, those lenses and categories are the reason, as we've been talking about, that we tend to get the Bible so wrong—they cause us to read it from the outside in rather than from the inside out. We evaluate the "rightness" of an idea through our dogma. That may be unintentional and happen on a purely subconscious level, but we do it nonetheless.

Some of us were trained in systematic theology in Bible college or seminary, and some of that can be helpful at times. But one of the things systematic theology teaches you to do is to subconsciously "check" your biblical interpretation against your prescribed theology or tradition, to make sure you're in the right place.

So you learn about chiasms, and it's amazing. You're comfortable diving in because when you hold the conclusions against the preapproved theological filter, they pass the test. You find these tools and use them—as long as they fit with your current lens.

But you're adding new tools to a toolbox that was already really heavy. And the fact is that *some of your old tools need to go* because they've gotten in the way of your growth. That development is natural. There isn't a single living thing that is healthy in a static state—including you.

Now, *not all your tools need to go*. Some tools are just fine and unique to you. And you're not going to chuck all your old tools wholesale; some of them you can get rid of today, and others you'll carry around until you're ready, until you've had enough conversations that convince you to let one go.

Some of these tools you've inherited from your forefathers, and you're simply not going to send them to the rummage sale. This is completely understandable. The tools we use are a way we honor our spiritual fathers and mothers. But you may find that you don't have to carry some of these things around anymore, weighing you down. Maybe you've got a great spot for them in your shop where you can display them and tell their story whenever somebody comes over.

But we need to realize that some of our tools may need to be reexamined. The hammer of Augustinian depravity is heavy and has done a lot of damage. A quick survey of early church history will show some disagreement about its place in our toolboxes, and we've found better tools that might be more effective and weigh a lot less.

A lot of the old tools we brought with us were made by the same brand, GnosticCraft™. History has shown that this toolmaker had some destructive practices, compromising the safety and effectiveness of their tools. We should consider this as we evaluate our toolbox.

Some of our tools are a little newer and, boy, were they innovative when they first came out! As the Middle Ages were going crazy, Thomas Aquinas paved the way for systematic theology and allowed the work of theology to stay relevant. It just so happens that we've gotten so used to using that drill, we've put holes in everything, so maybe we should consider how we're using it based on the job at hand.

As the world continued to develop and we got good at writing contracts and creating legal code, we found that if we combined this kind of thinking with systematic theology, we could create an entire infrastructure to support the world of theology. We explained penal substitutionary atonement with gusto and linked the discussion of justification, atonement, and salvation together like an art form. The problem is that as we've become more aware of the impact of that infrastructure and what we've done with it, we're increasingly turning to alternative theological energy sources, and that power grid may be less and less relevant moving forward. Maybe everything doesn't have to run off of classical Reformed theology all the time; maybe it shouldn't. Of course, the industry dependent on those tools will continue to double down and produce more and more of the same, but some of us may want to examine how the relationship of the Reformation interacts with our toolbox in both good and bad ways.

Again, it's important to note that not all these things need to go. There is a lot of beauty that my Reformed heritage brought me. The history of excellent theology is something I'm grateful for. But I do want to be able to examine my toolbox without overreacting in one direction or another.

And since those days, we've split into a million tool manufacturers, haven't we? It used to be just the big boys—GnosticCraft™, Calvin & Luther, DePope. But then the industry started getting all decentralized and everyone got in the game. So now you can head on down to the Harbor Freight of Protestantism and find a ton of cheaper options. It's really something.

But, again, that toolbox is heavy. And we need to pick the tools that are the most effective for the work we need to do today. As we get more and more used to them, we'll continue to learn to trust them, and as that trust grows, we'll start to see which other tools are no longer needed.

WHO IS MASTERING WHAT?

Our dogma, our absolute certainty in our own theological vantage point, suffocates a vibrant faith. It keeps our eyes on the ground, focused on maintaining the status quo, on keeping everything within the lines we've drawn. For all the chest-thumping we do about inspiration, it has seemed to me that we in the Western church have trusted not in the actual God who inspires the Text we study but in the definitions we've used and the ways we've explained and categorized that God and his Text.

We domesticated the Bible, slapped our trademark sticker on it—and only then did we start insisting on its grandeur.

I say "it has seemed to me" because I don't think the reality was nearly that systematized and intentional. I think this posture grew in us over time, as century after century's worth of dust and theological buildup caked over the original ideas.

For my entire career in teaching the Bible, I have been surrounded by people who carry themselves in a way that says that they have done it—they have "mastered" the Bible.

Apparently they've gotten enough education, hung out with enough of the right people, signed the right creed, preached enough sermons, prayed enough prayers—whatever it was—and they've gotten it. Whew! Finally!

Sometimes it's not individuals but movements, institutions, faith traditions, and other groups of people. Such tribal identities are highly effective in their ability to empower us and give us security, internal or otherwise.

They are also highly effective in their ability to deceive and give us a false sense of security.

But no matter what drives this belief, or the reasoning that's behind it, or the genesis of its existence, the idea seems completely backward.

We don't master the Text. Ever.

But if there's any truth to these convictions about the inspiration of the Text and the power of the God of the Bible, then this is true:

God is trying to master us.

And one of the ways he is doing this—in the gracious, graceful, compassionate, loving, wooing way that he does—is through this mysterious, deeper-than-any-waters, sacred text that we call the Bible.

The apostle John said in the closing verse of his Gospel,

> Jesus did many other things as well. If every one of them were written down, I suppose that even the whole world would not have room for the books that would be written.
>
> JOHN 21:25

Amen and amen, Rabbi John. I know this scares us because I know it scares me—to consider all the things that I do not know, let alone the things that I do know and do not yet understand.

But I believe in the power of God to write a better story than the one that my dogmatic theology has written. I believe in the power of asking good questions, and I believe that if I keep asking better and better questions, that journey will open me up to becoming the kind of person God wants me to be.

That last line—that's actually *it*, right?

Because this studying the inspired Word of God thing was never about figuring out all the answers. It was never about how if I worked hard enough and cracked the question code, I would master the Text.

This masterful thing that we call the Word of God was always given so that we would be changed. The reason our forefathers penned the stories and buried the treasures and constructed the chiasms was so that we would continue to look more and more like God with each passing generation.

There's no doubt that we've taken some big steps backward and lost our way, like the famous Prodigal Son. But this was never about the theological inheritance that we squandered in a faraway land. This was always about whether we would be content to head back to our Father's house and allow ourselves to be found.

RESOURCES REFERENCED

Searching for Sunday and *Evolving in Monkey Town* by Rachel Held Evans

Out of Sorts by Sarah Bessey

Unfettered and *The Vulnerable Pastor* by Mandy Smith

FOR FURTHER STUDY

anything (and everything) by Brené Brown (TED talks, books, etc.)

The Sacred Overlap by J. R. Briggs

Everything Is Spiritual by Rob Bell

How (Not) to Speak of God and *The Fidelity of Betrayal* by Peter Rollins

HAGAH

*Committing to Never Stop
Devouring the Word*

If the power of this journey lies in the God who inspires the Text—if the goal of this journey *isn't* amassing the most answers before we die—then I believe we need to talk about one more word and idea before we are done.

The Hebrew word *hagah*.

It shows up in a handful of places, but the best place to start is in Isaiah:

This is what the LORD says to me:

"As a lion *growls*,
     a great lion over its prey—

and though a whole band of shepherds
  is called together against it,
it is not frightened by their shouts
  or disturbed by their clamor—
so the LORD Almighty will come down
  to do battle on Mount Zion
    and on its heights."

ISAIAH 31:4, EMPHASIS ADDED

The Hebrew word for "growl" is *hagah*. It's a case of ono-matopoeia, where a word sounds like the thing it references. When you say it, you have to roll the *g* sound in the middle, and if you want to have fun with it, you let the sound hang for a while.

The word references the noise that a lion makes while hunching over a fresh kill—not a loud roar of dominance but a low rumble of satisfaction—and a warning to all the gathering hyenas that this lion has no intention of sharing the meal.

She intends to eat it. All of it. Every fiber and sinew.

Ha—gggggggggg—aaaaaahhhh.

The passage in Isaiah depicts this scene perfectly. Here's a lion that has just killed a sheep from the flock. The shepherds have gathered to exterminate this threat, but the lion sits over its prey and says, *Not until I'm done.*

Hagah also refers to the cooing of a dove or the roll of thunder.[1] The word brings with it a deep, rolling, grounded intention. Because of this, it gets translated a few different ways. Another one of my favorite uses of *hagah* is in Psalm 1:

> Blessed is the one
>   who does not walk in step with the wicked
> or stand in the way that sinners take
>   or sit in the company of mockers,
> but whose delight is in the law of the Lord,
>   and who meditates on his law day and night.
> That person is like a tree planted by streams
>   of water,
>   which yields its fruit in season
> and whose leaf does not wither—
>   whatever they do prospers.

PSALM 1:1-3

Could you guess where the word *hagah* shows up? Believe it or not, *hagah* is what gets translated as "meditate" here.

Now, I don't believe it's a bad translation. I just think we bring a bad word association to the passage. Most of us would think of a kind of stillness when we read the word *meditate*, right? We might picture sitting with Scripture, quietly reflecting on it in isolation, waiting on the voice of God. We'd get that perfect Instagram moment with a cappuccino on the porch with the sunrise and an open Bible (#blessed).

And yes, the Bible certainly has much to say about silence and reflection—there are words and expressions elsewhere in the Text that point to those things. Contemplative practices are a meaningful way to meet with God. I said earlier that Sabbath and solitude were part of the means God used to change my life. Silence and contemplation are still where I often experience God's abiding presence. I'm a huge advocate for these spiritual practices and don't want to downplay them at all.

But the practice of reflective stillness is not what is being referenced here.

When this psalm proclaims blessing on the person "whose delight is in the law of the LORD, and who meditates on [it] day and night," the psalmist is not thinking about an Instagram photo of someone on their back patio, an open Bible and a perfect cup of coffee before them, the sunrise casting rays over the whole scene.

The psalmist is writing about something like rolling thunder. Or a lion that has just sat down for a spiritual meal. This blessed person is the one who sits over their Bible, their scroll, their memorized verses—likely even with other people—intending to get every fiber and sinew out of the Word and suck the marrow out of its bones.

A TREE OF DEATH

But this psalm gets even more intriguing because there's some Jewish discussion about what kind of tree this person is like in Psalm 1. It would seem to be the same tree that Jeremiah speaks of in Jeremiah 17:

This is what the LORD says:

"Cursed is the one who trusts in man,
 who draws strength from mere flesh
 and whose heart turns away from the LORD.
That person will be like a bush in the wastelands;
 they will not see prosperity when it comes.
They will dwell in the parched places of the
  desert,
 in a salt land where no one lives.

"But blessed is the one who trusts in the LORD,
 whose confidence is in him.
They will be like a tree planted by the water
 that sends out its roots by the stream.
It does not fear when heat comes;
 its leaves are always green.
It has no worries in a year of drought
 and never fails to bear fruit."

JEREMIAH 17:5-8

The wording is so similar that one biblical botanist, Nogah Hareuveni (considered by many to be the modern era's greatest authority on biblical botany), said there is very little question about what tree is being discussed in Psalm 1. To learn his reasoning, we'll work backward.

In the Jeremiah passage, the first tree mentioned is that of the cursed one, the one who trusts in his own strength. This is usually translated as "bush" because of the unique Hebrew word. This Hebrew word also speaks to a very particular desert shrub, known as the *arar*.

The *arar* bush can be found in some of the driest places in the Negev desert. This bush is striking in its visual appearance—bright green and robust looking. On the bush grow grapefruit-sized "fruit," which is also bright green and seemingly luscious. When you see one, you immediately wonder if it might be edible or otherwise useful. Everything about this bush seems delightful from the outside.

You walk over and pick a fruit from the tree. When you hold it in your hand, it's surprisingly light. Maybe the juicy payoff isn't quite what you think it will be. So you open the outer husk of this fruit to the sound of *pop!*—and are amazed to find that it's completely empty. There is nothing inside the husk; it's barren and useless.

Not only this, but from the outer husk begins to leak a white milky substance, which happens to be toxic. *This tree looks good from the outside, but the reality is a dangerous letdown.*

This leads Hareuveni to conclude that the tree in the next paragraph, the tree of the blessed one, should obviously be in direct juxtaposition to the *arar*. To those ends, Hareuveni says that the tree of the blessed one is the Palestinian acacia tree.[2]

Many people are familiar with this desert tree, which is sparse looking with a flat top, shaped like an umbrella. Different varieties of these trees can be found all over the world, especially on the continent of Africa. Even though this tree is visibly sparse, it is far from useless.

In the region of Palestine, the Bedouins have often called the acacia tree the "gift of the desert." The tree is unbelievably good at providing shade when most needed. The salt content of the tree absorbs moisture from the air, which makes its shade ever so slightly cooler than shade from other trees.

The wood of the acacia tree provides strong building materials for the Bedouin people, and its wood burns longer and hotter than wood from other trees, making it an efficient resource for fires and cooking. The sap of the tree is believed to have medicinal properties, and the tree's tiny pods are nutritious for livestock. A Bedouin told one of my teachers that one kilo of boiled acacia pods could feed a camel for a week.

But here is the other striking thing about acacia trees in this region: You find them growing at the bottom of wadis that open into the wilderness. A wadi is like a desert canyon. In that region, the rainy season comes and lasts for just over two months. Because the desert has a hard time accepting the water, it pushes it right out and away. When it rains heavily, this can cause massive desert floods, which happen to be the number one cause of death in the deserts of Israel.

Wadi floods can travel down these canyons for miles and miles until the wadi ends, opening into the wilderness (examples of this would be the few hundred yards between the western coast of the Dead Sea and the impending Judaean mountains). Wherever wadis come to an end, you will find clumps of acacia trees because that is where the water races and then comes to rest and pools during floods.

Now, some wadis get rain and flood every year, but other wadis only flood when they experience the right conditions. You'd assume that the acacia trees in drier wadis wouldn't survive, that they would die after years of drought. But in fact, these trees go dormant—and should they get a rainy season, even years later, they spring to life.

I've seen this firsthand when I've taught this lesson on study tours to Israel every other year. I have my favorite spots and the trees that I like to use. For a few trips I used the same dead-looking acacia tree found in the bottom of one of my favorite wadis. And then one trip a few years ago, I visited that same tree, and it was green (not overly green, but green), with fresh pods growing on it. I know my students were a little confused over my excitement about that less-than-impressive tree.

Acacia trees, I have been told, can sit for eight, nine, even twelve years or more without rain and still—given the right conditions—spring to life.

And now we understand what Hareuveni was trying to point out. Jeremiah is purposely juxtaposing these two desert trees. Deserts are part of the human experience. Of that there is very little doubt. But our response to the deserts is not universal. Some of us respond with our own strength and abilities. Those folks often come across with a sense of worldly wisdom, looking like they have it together. They look green and impressive, like they're bearing fruit and shining in the middle of a wilderness season. But inside, they are full of emptiness and death.

What of those who follow the counterintuitive way, trusting God in their deserts? They may come off as dead and unimpressive. Nothing about them tells you that they have anything to offer—but given the right conditions, when the rain comes, they spring to life. As Jeremiah says, they do not worry in drought, because they never fail to bear fruit. And they are the "gift of the desert" to those who live there.

THE *HAGAH* TREE

With that information, we head back to Psalm 1.

> Blessed is the one
>   who does not walk in step with the wicked
> or stand in the way that sinners take
>   or sit in the company of mockers,
> but whose *delight* is in the law of the LORD,
>   and who *meditates* on his law day and night.
> That person is like a tree planted by *streams of water*,
>   which yields its fruit *in season*
> and whose leaf does not wither—
>   whatever they do prospers.

PSALM I:I-3, EMPHASIS ADDED

Psalm 1 speaks of a person who understands wisdom and where it is found. This person does not live by sight and what the eyes can see. They have heard the voice of the great Desert Shepherd and the voice of their ancestors as they have asked for the ancient way. They have trusted in this evidence and decided that they will find their delight in the law of the Lord. Because of this, they resolutely set their mind on *hagah*-ing the Text.

The psalmist says that these trees are planted by "streams of water," but many Jewish minds have pointed out that this phrase can refer to "rushing waters," which should now remind us of wadi floods. And this means that bearing fruit "in its season" refers not to perfect rhythms that happen like clockwork but to those "appointed times" that you don't even see coming—but that come from a deeply rooted life that, when the time is right, yields fruit.

I remember coming back from my first trip to Israel in 2008 after learning about this for the first time. I had been mentored for years by those who were deeply committed to contemplative practices, which, as I stated earlier, I will be forever grateful for. I bless God for what they taught me.

I knew that these practices would be important for me because I naturally gravitate toward the cerebral, book-learning, and thinking side of my brain. In other words, I gravitate to things where I can lean on my own strength. These are things that I can control, that I can test my competence on. These are things where I know that I can look good and have it covered.

Just like an *arar* bush.

So I wanted to discipline myself to trust in the Lord

better. I poured myself into prayer and contemplation, just like my mentors told me to, and I continue to do so to this day. This hasn't come easily. But I remain committed to these things because I have to find ways to cling to the mysterious power of God in my life.

However, when I came back from that trip to Israel, I had been given a new gift that provided such a way. It was not the Bible as an act of study. It was not the "textbook" Scripture that we all complained about in Bible college.

It was the discipline of *hagah*.

You don't engage in this discipline to learn more data. The practice of *hagah* isn't something that you do so that you can be tested on it. No, this is a practice that creates space for the mysterious power of God to go to work. I tell my students that there is an indirect promise in the Scripture that if you create space for God, *He will fill it*. *Hagah* is that practice. I spend time meditating on the law of the Lord, putting God's words in me, and somehow, in ways that I don't fully understand and can't explain, God uses them to do their thing.

Another favorite passage of mine that I believe speaks to this is from Isaiah 55:

As the rain and the snow
    come down from heaven,
and do not return to it
    without watering the earth
and making it bud and flourish,

> so that it yields seed for the sower and bread for
>   the eater,
> so is my word that goes out from my mouth:
>   It will not return to me empty,
> but will accomplish what I desire
>   and achieve the purpose for which I sent it.
>
> ISAIAH 55:10-11

There is something truly mysterious and unique about God's words. This mysterious power isn't a tool that you stick in your toolbox because it's not something that you use—this is something that uses you.

It's one of many ways that we learn to trust in the Lord.

A FINAL WORD

I share all this as an invitation to remember that nothing in this book matters if it's not infused with the power and presence of God. I have been consistently frustrated by centuries' worth of church history that has continued to correct this creed or that system. We've studied and thought and philosophized until we're blue in the face. Along the way, we've actually come up with some pretty amazing thoughts, and God has worked in spite of us in so many ways. I'm thankful for that.

We've also gotten a lot of stuff really wrong.

Sometimes these details are relatively insignificant and harmless. Assumptions about clothing in biblical culture or the age of the disciples might be examples. But sometimes those things have led to some pretty destructive readings of the Scriptures and have hurt an awful lot of people.

These things matter. It's why I wrote this book. And I hope this book has given some insights and tools that will help all of us ask better questions of the Bible and steward this incredible gift of the Text for our world—for this generation and for future ones. But if all we do is correct our toolbox and update the operating system, and we still don't learn to trust in the Lord, we'll just continue to be an *arar* bush in a barren wasteland.

I'm praying that as our commitment to the Text is revitalized, there will be a newfound fire in our bones—and just as Jeremiah said, that if we say we will not speak of God again, his word will become a fire that we cannot contain (Jeremiah 20:9). I'm praying that we'll get to know the God who breathed life and power into the pages of that Bible and that this experiential and mysterious knowing will empower us to be the partners God is looking for. And that his Word will go forward, that we will bear fruit in season, and that none of this will return void.

No matter what we learn about biblical history and literary tools, no matter what they dig out of the dirt or what we understand, I pray that you and I will stand together among the acacia trees in the new Garden of Eden.

Hopefully we have discovered that we are companions on this journey. Maybe we didn't set out with the intention of needing each other, but we met along the way nonetheless.

There's more ahead to explore, and I'm encouraged by the company. Others have gotten here long before we did and helped pave the way. There are others coming behind us who are hoping we'll do the same.

Will you join me?

May you be equipped to read the Bible
with a more historically grounded hermeneutic.

May you not be afraid of the questions,
and may you ask many more.

May you create a space for God as you love him with
all your heart and all your soul and all your might.

And may he fill it.

Acknowledgments

I will start by thanking the awesome team at NavPress. So many people helped make this book what it is. To David Zimmerman, thanks for believing in this work and giving it a chance. To Elizabeth Schroll, for making me sound intelligent (seriously, how many times can I use the same word in a single chapter?). And to Caitlyn Carlson, who went above and beyond for this new author who had no idea what he was doing.

Thank you to Alyssa Cordova and Tim Peterson. You convinced me that I could write a book and planted the seeds of this project, when I'm pretty sure I would have talked myself out of it.

To those mentors who have shaped me into the person I am today, who insisted that Jesus was the most important thing and that loving others like him was my most important job in ministry. Special thanks to Bill Westfall, Steve Edwards, and Brian Vriesman.

To J.R. Briggs, for your friendship and training and little words of encouragement that made me feel like I belonged here. That is priceless, and I am honored.

To my teammates and the board of directors at Impact Campus Ministries, for being a group of people that make me love my job.

Reed and Austin, two of the best friends that a guy could ever ask for: Thank you for your friendship. Austin, for never letting me go a week without checking in. Reed, for always pushing me to go where I'd rather not. You both make me a better person.

To every student in my ministry who ever opened your eyes wide and said, "WHAT!?" To every graduate who left daring to love others well. You have inspired me relentlessly with your unique faith. To every single listener, supporter, and partner of BEMA and what we do: Thank you for all the thank-you emails and stories and questions. I do not deserve you, but I am so very thankful to God for the gift you all are to me.

Finally, to the last, most deserving mentions . . .

Thank you to Brent Billings. Without you, there would likely be none of this. For the ways that you serve and the ways that you make everything that I touch beyond perfect. And for being such a trustworthy and selfless partner.

Thank you to my children. You are my inspiration in so many incredible ways; I love who you are and everything about what you are becoming. Obviously, Becky. You are my love, my favorite; there is nobody like you. Brené Brown has said, "Never underestimate the power of being seen—it's exhausting to keep working against yourself when someone truly sees you and loves you."[1]

And thanks be to Jesus, who has never abandoned me and who never lets me believe I am any less than what he believes me to be.

Notes

CHAPTER 1 | SEEING THE TEXT IN CONTEXT

1. Brené Brown, *Rising Strong: How the Ability to Reset Transforms the Way We Live, Love, Parent, and Lead* (New York: Random House, 2017), 79.
2. McLaren touches on this in *A New Kind of Christian: A Tale of Two Friends on a Spiritual Journey* (San Francisco: Jossey-Bass, 2001).
3. Gary M. Burge, *The Bible and the Land: Uncover the Ancient Culture, Discover Hidden Meanings* (Grand Rapids, MI: Zondervan, 2009), 11.

CHAPTER 2 | PLAYING WITH BOTH HANDS

1. That talk was given at Twin Falls Reformed Church (Twin Falls, ID) in the fall of 2007.
2. For a visual presentation of the same content, see the show notes for this episode in your podcast app.

CHAPTER 3 | LETTING TORAH READ YOU

1. For a deeper dive on seven different kinds of chiasmus, I recommend reading Kenneth E. Bailey, a renowned New Testament literary scholar. He gave a great breakdown of these in his work on the Gospel of Luke, *Poet & Peasant / Through Peasant Eyes* (combined volume).
2. Rabbi David Fohrman's online academy at alephbeta.org is full of video presentations that aid in our ability to see this literary device at work.
3. This is a simplified version of an image in Rabbi David Fohrman, *Genesis: A Parsha Companion* (New Milford, CT: Aleph Beta Press, 2019), 48. Permission was granted by the copyright owner to use this modified version here.

4. For more on ancient flood narratives, see https://www.metmuseum.org /toah/hd/flod/hd_flod.htm.

5. Abraham was eighty-six years old when Ishmael was born (Genesis 16:16) and one hundred years old when Isaac was born (Genesis 21:5). It would have taken at least a year for Isaac to be weaned.

6. For more on this, see https://www.alephbeta.org/playlist/akedah-meaning ?video=child-sacrifice-in-the-torah.

7. For more on the conquest narrative as a genre, see https://www.thegospel coalition.org/themelios/review/ancient-conquest-accounts-a-study-in -ancient-near-eastern-and-biblical-history-writing-jsot-supplement-98; https:// biblicalhistoricalcontext.com/conquest-of-canaan/joshua-10-and-11-genre -and-the-common-narrative-structure; and Ian Douglas Wilson, "Conquest and Form: Narrativity in Joshua 5–11 and Historical Discourse in Ancient Judah," *Harvard Theological Review* 106, no. 3 (July 2013): 309–29.

8. Ray Vander Laan identifies this outline in "A Covenant Guarantee," accessed May 20, 2022, https://www.thattheworldmayknow.com /a-covenant-guarantee. Section labels and explanations are my own.

9. There's a very helpful, if not overwhelming, resource online that serves as a library to Jewish tradition at sefaria.org.

10. For more on the Talmud, see https://www.sefaria.org/What_is_the_Talmud %2C_I_What_is_the_Talmud%3F%2C_1_Bible_and_Talmud.3?lang=en.

11. Ilana Kurshan, *If All the Seas Were Ink: A Memoir* (New York: St. Martin's Press, 2017), 289.

12. Fohrman is an orthodox Jewish teacher teaching about the Torah from a Jewish (and non-Christian) perspective. Alpha Beta Academy offers a great opportunity to see how the Jewish mind engages these Jewish books. It is also one of the places where I have learned about numerous chiasms and how they function in the Torah.

CHAPTER 4 | HISTORY AS PROPHECY

1. Abraham Joshua Heschel, *The Prophets* (New York: Perennial Classics, 2001).

2. Ira Spar, "Sennacherib and Jerusalem," The Met, November 24, 2014, https://www.metmuseum.org/exhibitions/listings/2014/assyria-to-iberia /blog/posts/sennacherib-and-jerusalem.

3. Hélène M. Dallaire touches on this in "Taking the Land by Force: Divine Violence in Joshua," in *Wrestling with the Violence of God: Soundings in the Old Testament*, ed. M. Daniel Carroll R. and J. Blair Wilgus (Winona Lake, IN: Eisenbrauns, 2015), 60–61.

4. Peter Enns, *The Bible Tells Me So: Why Defending Scripture Has Made Us Unable to Read It* (New York: HarperOne, 2014), 63, 231.

CHAPTER 5 | READING WISDOM WITH WISDOM

1. Reed Dent, sermon called "Wisdom" (Campus Christian Fellowship at Truman State University, August 28, 2019). Quoted with permission.
2. Rachel Held Evans, *Inspired: Slaying Giants, Walking on Water, and Loving the Bible Again* (Nashville: Nelson Books, 2018), 98.
3. Reed Dent, sermon called "Wisdom" (Campus Christian Fellowship at Truman State University, August 28, 2019). Quoted with permission.
4. Reed Dent, sermon called "*Chokmah*" (Campus Christian Fellowship at Truman State University, August 30, 2017). Quoted with permission.

CHAPTER 6 | PUTTING THE PROPHETS IN THEIR PLACE

1. His book *The Prophets* is an excellent read for anyone seeking to understand the difference between the prophets and any other author in Scripture.
2. Walter Brueggemann, *Out of Babylon* (Nashville: Abingdon Press, 2010).

CHAPTER 7 | THE GOOD NEWS ABOUT THE GOSPELS

1. For more on Beth Shemesh, see Ray Vander Laan, That the World May Know series, Lesson 4 of Volume 1, *Promised Land* (Grand Rapids, MI: Zondervan, 2015), DVD.
2. Quoted in Plato, *Theaetetus* (London: Penguin Books, 2004), 47.
3. For more on the Zealots, see Richard A. Horsley with John S. Hanson, *Bandits, Prophets, and Messiahs: Popular Movements in the Time of Jesus* (Harrisburg, PN: Trinity Press International, 1999).
4. This translation of the Greek is transcribed from my audio recording of a lecture by Ray Vander Laan that I attended.
5. M. D. Goulder, *The Evangelists' Calendar: A Lectionary Explanation of the Development of Scripture* (London: SPCK, 1972).
6. The end of this chapter lists continued resources to study, but most of what we know about Hillel and Shammai is drawn out of the Mishnah, the Talmud, and other pieces of Jewish midrash.
7. While the four levels of Jewish interpretation, "PaRDeS"—*peshat, remez, derash*, and *sod*—were not articulated for almost another thousand years, the principles are clearly in play throughout Mishnaic and Talmudic history. These principles of allusion are the building blocks of Jewish hermeneutics, especially as it relates to parables. Some teachers, like Dwight Prior, suggested that these principles may have gone by other names, such as *keshers* (which means "knot" and could have referred to the Jewish concept known as "stringing pearls"). A deeper dive into PaRDeS can be heard in episode 110 of *The BEMA Podcast* and read in the attached show notes.

8. Some of these principles would be *gezerah shavah*, the art of tying two unrelated passages together because they use the same expression or phrase; Jesus does this with the money changers in the Temple courts when he attaches two unrelated passages from Isaiah and Jeremiah together to make an ingenious teaching point. Another example would be *kal va'chomer*, where Jesus used the rabbinic principle of exaggerated comparison to make his point; this is usually seen with the phrase *how much more* ("if this is how God clothes the grass of the field . . . how much more will he clothe you") or in cultural comparison like the parable of the talents (making the king synonymous with Herod's son Antipas from one perspective and Archelaus from the other).

CHAPTER 8 | LEARNING ABOUT THE LETTERS
1. Brian Zahnd, *Beauty Will Save the World: Rediscovering the Allure and Mystery of Christianity* (Lake Mary, FL: Charisma House, 2012), 210.
2. Kenneth E. Bailey, *Poet and Peasant and Through Peasant Eyes: A Literary-Cultural Approach to the Parables in Luke* (Grand Rapids, MI: Eerdmans, 2000).
3. Brian D. McLaren, *A Generous Orthodoxy: Why I Am a Missional, Evangelical, Post/Protestant, Liberal/Conservative, Mystical/Poetic, Biblical, Charismatic/Contemplative, Fundamentalist/Calvinist, Anabaptist/Anglican, Methodist, Catholic, Green, Incarnational, Depressed-yet-Hopeful, Emergent, and Unfinished Christian* (Grand Rapids, MI: Youth Specialties, 2004), 206.

CHAPTER 9 | APOCALYPTIC REVELATIONS
1. Bible Hub, "Strong's 602. *apokalupsis*," accessed May 20, 2022, https://biblehub.com/greek/602.htm.
2. Rob Bell in "The Original Guerilla Theatre" (a video production of the Poets, Prophets, and Preachers conference, July 2009, Grand Rapids, MI).

A FINAL WORD | *HAGAH*
1. See, for example, Gesenius's Hebrew-Chaldee Lexicon entry: https://www.blueletterbible.org/lexicon/h1897/niv/wlc/0-1.
2. I don't recall which of his books Nogah Hareuveni mentions this in; see *Ecology in the Bible* (1974), *Tree and Shrub in Our Biblical Heritage* (1984), and *Desert and Shepherd in Our Biblical Heritage* (1991).

ACKNOWLEDGMENTS
1. Brené Brown, *Braving the Wilderness: The Quest for True Belonging and the Courage to Stand Alone* (New York: Random House, 2019), 17.